To my good friend Ayana!
May you laugh forever!
4-30-16

I CAN *Laugh* AGAIN

From the Valley of Grief to a Glimpse of Heaven

Chloé Taylor Brown

a Memoir by
Chloé Taylor Brown

authorHOUSE®

AuthorHouse™
1663 Liberty Drive
Bloomington, IN 47403
www.authorhouse.com
Phone: 1 (800) 839-8640

Published by AuthorHouse 12/01/2015

ISBN: 978-1-5049-2783-3 (sc)
ISBN: 978-1-5049-2782-6 (e)

Library of Congress Control Number: 2015912579

Print information available on the last page.

Other books by Chloé Taylor Brown:
Getting Ready Chloé-Style: Perfecting Your Authentic Image
Determine Your Ideal: Lifestyle Enhancement Workbook
Girl-Swag: A Global Girl's Curriculum for Personal
Development & Lifestyle Enhancement

Find out more about Chloé Taylor Brown:
www.thechloeXperience.com
chloe@thechloeXperience.com
Connect with Chloé on Social Media
Twitter @ChloeTBrown
Facebook Chloé Taylor Brown
LinkedIn Chloé Taylor Brown
Instagram Chloé Taylor Brown

Baby Justin's First Birthday

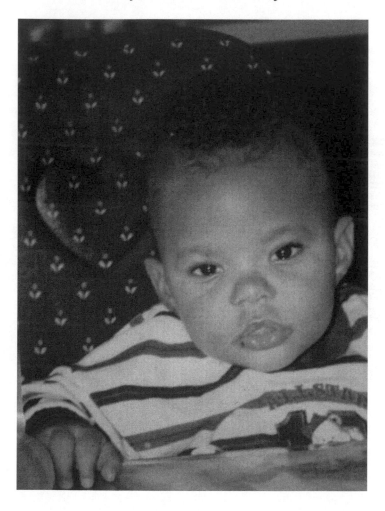

DEDICATION

This memoir is dedicated to anyone who has ever lost a loved one. It represents a part of my life story and an even greater part of my heart. I feel brave enough to share it with you now, as I believe it may encourage someone else today. I also dedicate this book to Rick, Jade, Taylor and Joshua Brown.

—Chloé Taylor Brown

TABLE OF CONTENTS

Foreword

I Can Laugh Again is all about love. It's truly an evocative story about love's essential and enduring qualities. Chloé Taylor Brown bares her soul—her dreams, hopes, losses, pains, and gains—in a riveting account you cannot read without taking part yourself in her transformation. The impetus for the narrative involves the tragic death of her nearly four-year-old son, Justin; but Justin's life is just the stepping stone, if you will, upon which she reminisces throughout her life's journey, blazing a path from rural Mississippi to the highest strata of the world of fashion. In the end, as we've shared her passage from heartbreak to triumph, she gives us a glimpse of heaven.

My long-time friend Chloé paints a vivid and easily recognizable map to finding a practical faith. No matter the obstacles, in the end she assures us that we can trust a Power greater than ourselves to get us through, with more grace than we ever imagined.

You'll find yourself immersed in more than one love story: a mother's abiding love for her children; Chloé's undying love for her husband, Rick, and his deep love for her; their constant love for their children and their families; and the outpouring of love from their spiritual family all over the world. Above all, there is the prevailing Power of God's redeeming Love.

I encourage you, dear reader, to accept the priceless, immeasurable, and timeless gift of reading this book. It is my prayer that you will encounter the universal language of the heart, which this memoir brings so poignantly to the surface. You'll surely gain a new appreciation for the simple values that make life worth living.

Enough said by me. Go ahead and trust your heart: Discover and rediscover the unending Power of Love.

—Carl A. Lee

INTRODUCTION

Years ago, I experienced a paradigm crash. Everything in my world shattered into more than a million little pieces—following the death of Justin, my youngest child at the time. Almost every decision my husband and I made then seemed wrong. This is because we were operating from such a low level in every aspect of our lives—physically, mentally, emotionally, and, most of all, spiritually. After months and years of grief and spiritual counseling, more years of personal development, coaching, and transformational work, plus the support of a circle of wonderful friends and loving family members who stuck with me, I kept the faith that there was just a bit more I could become, and more I could offer to the world. I began to slowly feel well enough to reevaluate my life and my values. This was not easy, and it took a while, but it certainly restored me, just a little more each day. In order for me to move forward, I knew I had to determine a new *ideal* for my life, and no matter how much pain I was in, it seemed the process had to start right where I was—with me.

Who am I? I asked myself. *Where do I go from here? Who do I want to become? What can I do and share with other people from my own life experiences, that actually matters?*

A *determined ideal* is much bigger than a goal, although goals are vital in accomplishing your ideal. A determined ideal is a clear, multidimensional, holographic picture we hold in our mind's eye of who we are, and how we want to live our life, combined with a step-by-step plan to help us make it happen. My husband and I had both had our own individual plans before our paradigm crash; we created them in college and in turn we made the life of our dreams together. But after the crash, I was drifting and losing most of my energy and power. My energy became fragmented and dispersed into insignificant meaningless tasks. My life became filled with a whole lot of busy-ness, adding up to nothing.

During the darkest time of my life, what I missed most was *laughter*. The lack of it was destroying me and my family. My most memorable authentic prayer at the time was, "*Please God! Just let me laugh again!*" I loved my own laughter, and I knew it filled our home with a certain assurance.

Once I allowed myself to actually laugh out loud, and not feel a sense of guilt—and even giggle—I started getting my life-energy back. The laughter actually started to increase my energy and bring some of my power back to me. I was finally able to *be present* again. I started getting out of my head and back into my heart, which led me back to my life. I began taking chances on myself again and hired a transformational life coach to help me, because I knew I could do better; and I was ready to do the work.

I hope my story will help you along on your own journey. In my own way, I've learned to encourage myself daily. These inspiring words came to me recently, and now I give them to you: *Everything that you've been doing has been practiced and mastered. Now you're ready to create your masterpiece.*

CHAPTER 1

Justin

I heard the happy chirping of birds through our bedroom window. It was delightful, like birds in love singing to each other. *If only I could sing*, I thought, *I'd sing love songs to my husband.* And even though I couldn't carry a tune in a bucket if my life depended upon it, the thought intrigued me. Rick wasn't home, though—he had slipped out of bed early and taken the children to breakfast. A contented smile crossed my lips when I realized they weren't there. My husband knew me well. I was pleased to have the house to myself.

It was Sunday, the day before Labor Day. Our family had had a wonderful, exhilarating summer, and had actually been a part of history by going to many of the events and celebrations for the 1996 Atlanta Summer Olympic Games. However, all of this was behind us now and there were only three more days of real summer left before school would start again.

"I want these days to be calm and peaceful," I had told Rick the night before. "I just need a little bit of R and R before school starts."

1

I loved the quiet house and the stillness of the early morning. My thoughts could escape clearly, resounding through the air, yet always finding their way back to me, larger, more complete.

I had been accused many times by quite a number of people of being an idealist, as though it was a character flaw which needed fixing. Yes, I was full of dreams and hopes, and I allowed my ideas and thoughts to induce wonderful spiritual highs. This morning's backdrop was perfect. I had been enraptured by the bright sunlight coming through the bedroom windows, and drawn into the charm of the singing birds, which made beautiful background music for my meditation. I craved this state of mind and didn't want anything to interfere with my flow, but feeling dehydrated I desperately needed something to drink. I forced myself up from the bed, *Walk softly*, I told myself, as I walked down the long hallway to the kitchen, trying not to interrupt the flow. I was really taking advantage of my time alone.

I made myself a pot of Earl Grey tea, and feeling special, I poured it into the silver teapot Jade and Taylor had gotten me the previous Mother's Day.

Use your Spode teacup and saucer, my subconscious whispered. *What's the point of having fine china if you never use it*? I took out the teacup and saucer, placed them on the breakfast tray along with the silver teapot and several packets of sugar, and quickly returned to my bedroom. Still, I walked softly.

Wonderful! The birds are still singing. I sat on the floor, right in the middle of a pile of books, magazines and photo contact sheets I had spread out the night before. Smiling and reminiscing, I picked up the contact sheets as I sipped my tea.

Several weeks earlier our family had done a photo shoot for one of my many projects. Looking at the contact sheets, I found myself laughing out loud. Justin, our baby boy, had done everything he could think of to avoid cooperating. He stuck his tongue out, pulled his ears, blew kisses to the camera, hugged his dad, and slapped his sister several times. After all of the drama and confusion, Tom was such a wonderful photographer he still got lots of great shots. I was enamored by the images in front of me as I held the negatives up to the light. "Look how beautiful and happy we look," I whispered. "It's going to be difficult to choose just one."

I stayed in my bedroom all morning sipping tea, reminiscing, and counting my blessings. I was still in the flow when I heard the door slam.

"Mommy! Where are you Mommy? We're home."

My time was up—back to reality.

Rick returned with the boys just after lunch. Justin ran to me grinning, clutching a bag, which contained his favorite food.

"I see Justin talked you into going to McDonald's again."

"Yeah, he and Taylor wanted to go." Rick was guilty. "A small bag of French fries won't hurt him."

"Whatever," I said sarcastically, knowing very well a small bag of French fries every time anyone passed by a McDonald's just might hurt the child. But Justin was adamant. There were two McDonald's in our neighborhood, and he knew when we were in the vicinity of either of them.

Rick had taken Jade to Sophia's house, her best friend. "I'll pick her up before dinner," he promised.

I was left standing in the kitchen, twirling my hair. Dinner! I hadn't thought of dinner. *What should I plan for dinner?* The phone rang, startling me.

"Hello," impulsively I answered, but immediately I remembered my earlier promise to myself. I didn't want to be bothered with the phone today; it interfered with my flow in a major way.

"Hello Chloé. It's Lena."

I kicked myself. Lena was in town from New York visiting her mother. This was her third call. I had had every intention of calling her back, but this was not a good time to talk. I just wasn't in the mood. I was really mad at myself now for answering the phone, especially since she wanted me to help a friend of hers become a model. I didn't mind helping young girls, but modeling was the last thing I wanted to talk about right then. *Why did I answer this phone?* I punched my thigh, in anger toward myself. As I continued to speak with her, I saw Justin and Taylor marching out the back door. Only staying outside for a couple of minutes, they came back inside. Justin still clung to his bag of French fries as he continued to walk through the house. He waved to me with his free hand. I wanted to talk to the boys, not Lena. I looked around the room and up toward the ceiling, rolling my eyes.

Finally, the conversation ended. I promised myself, *I won't answer it anymore today*. Breathing a sigh of contentment, I walked into the library where Rick and Taylor were watching the Braves game on television.

"Who was that?" Rick asked.

4

"Lena," I answered irritably. "She's at her mom's house and she wants me to meet one of her girlfriends today to help her with modeling. She acted like she was going to die if she didn't talk to me today."

As I spoke I noticed Justin wasn't sitting in the library with them. "Where is Justin?" I asked nonchalantly, expecting Rick or Taylor to say, "He's over there," or "He's in here." Instead Rick replied, "I don't know." Casually I strolled out of the library, leaving Taylor and Rick watching the game while I looked for Justin.

I walked through the large family room looking from side to side calling, "Justin? Where are you, Justin?" He didn't answer. I continued into the kitchen, calling his name. There was no answer. I turned around in the kitchen and went to the back stairs and called up to his room, pausing, waiting for him to answer. Still, there was no answer. I walked back to the kitchen and out the back door. Standing on the high deck I looked straight out to the play area to see if he was swinging. Justin loved to swing, but he wasn't there either. I glanced to my right to see if he was riding his Big Wheel. It was there, but he wasn't on it. I walked to the edge of the deck and looked down. There he was. Justin was facedown, floating in the pool. My worst nightmare had just begun.

Without thinking, I ran from the deck, pulling one shoe off, then the other. I had on blue jeans and a tee shirt. It didn't matter, nothing did except saving my baby. I dove into the pool, pulling Justin out seconds later. Running with him in my arms, I screamed over and over, "Rick! Rick! Rick! Rick!" although it seemed no sound was coming out of my mouth. I stopped running. I needed to do something.

I placed Justin on the ground and slapped his little face. He looked sweet and peaceful. He didn't respond. I began giving him mouth-to-mouth resuscitation, a milky-white foam started to ooze out of his mouth and nose, but still there was no response.

By now my voice had registered to Rick and Taylor. They ran out of the kitchen door onto the deck. As I was bent down on my knees over Justin's limp body, I looked up at Rick. He was standing there, looking down at me, screaming, in slow motion it seemed. "Nooo, Baby. Nooo!"

He and Taylor ran down the steps and into the fenced pool area. I picked Justin up again and ran toward the house. Rick sprinted past me to call 911 but left the phone hanging from the receiver when I yelled, "We don't have time! We've got to go right now."

It took us six minutes to get to the Children's Hospital in our neighborhood. Before the car was stopped completely, I jumped out. Rick followed me, only putting the car in park, with Taylor following after him. As I rushed into the front door of the emergency room, the nurses and attendants immediately took Justin out of my arms. "What happened?" They begged, running down the corridor with him.

Horrified, we ran behind them crying, "He fell into the pool!"

They wouldn't let us go into the room where they had taken our baby boy; instead, a nurse led us to a small room that wasn't a waiting room. It was sterile and cold, with lots of stainless steel. This small room was only two doors down from where they worked on Justin, but it seemed as though it was in another building. A nice young man came in to give us what little information he had about Justin. He told us the doctors were doing everything they could right now. "When you brought your son in, he didn't have a heartbeat." My own heart seemed to stop.

Rick and I grabbed each other and held on. "They got a heartbeat, but they lost it." My heart stopped again. I could barely breathe. Rick and I had been very quiet up until now, but now we held onto each other and Taylor as we cried and waited for the young man to come back with more information. Yes, we waited, and hoped, for good news about Justin.

I looked down at Taylor and saw for the first time he was in shock; his entire forehead had been scratched. When he saw Justin lying on the ground and realized what had happened, he began running around the backyard in circles, digging his fingernails deep into his own little sweet face, drawing blood.

The young man came back, "The doctors have gotten a heartbeat."

"Praise the Lord!" Rick and I both looked up with tears in our eyes.

"You can't see your son right now, though. You have to wait until he is given a room in ICU." For the first time since I found Justin lying in the pool, I could breathe again. My baby was a fighter, and I knew he could survive this. He had been in ICU before and pulled through. Justin and I had gone through a lot together and I knew him. *He will make it. Stay strong for Justin*, I told myself.

I had forgotten my clothes were soaking wet until the young man who had been kind to us before handed me scrubs to wear. "Do you all want something to drink?" He offered us Cokes. All of a sudden, Rick and I looked at each other, "Jade!" There was a phone in the little room so we called Joe and Christina (her friend Sophia's parents) and asked them to bring our daughter to the hospital. Next, I phoned my sister Brenda, to tell her I was at the hospital and what had happened. I couldn't get the words out. Shocked, I tried again, but the words just wouldn't come. I heard Brenda inhale and exhale deeply. "Chloé, which child is it?"

"Justin." I cried uncontrollably for the first time.

"Chloé, I'll be right there."

As soon as I hung up the phone, I dialed the number for St. Jude Catholic Church. Unlike Jade and Taylor, Justin hadn't been baptized. I began to panic when the voice on the other end told me that Monsignor O'Conner wasn't there; but another priest arrived at the hospital within twenty minutes, prepared to baptize Justin. Brenda and the priest arrived at the same time, just as we were being led to Justin in ICU. We had been in the hospital now for nearly three hours. The priest wasn't from St. Jude, but everything about him was familiar. He went right over to Justin's bed and baptized him, "If your son died right now, or anytime from this point on, he would go straight to heaven." I looked down at Justin. *I don't want to hear anything about dying.*

"Mr. and Mrs. Brown," a nurse got our attention. "The doctor will be right with you." We hadn't spoken to a doctor the entire time we had been in the hospital. We held our breath as the doctor walked over to us.

CHAPTER 2

Marital Bliss

It was our tenth wedding anniversary. Rick held me affectionately in his arms. "I love you," he whispered. "You look absolutely fabulous tonight." A sly smile appeared on his face. "I had no idea that a pregnant woman could be so sexy, and have so much energy."

I was actually impressed myself. My energy level seemed to increase as the night passed. "And this dress!" He commented, spinning me around as he looked at me. Blushing, I snuggled closer to him. He was definitely my man, and we were more in love than we had ever been.

I designed the dress with my designer friend Vanessa, and it was definitely a showstopper. We laughed and giggled like schoolgirls as we decided to take advantage of my newly developed 36D bra size. "Show some cleavage, Girl," Vanessa insisted. "You know they're not going to last forever." The flamboyant, flirtatious side of me blurted out, "Okay, Girl, I'll do it!"

The dress was red, with spaghetti straps which crisscrossed in the back. Layers and layers of silk chiffon fell from the empire-cut waist.

As Rick spun me around on the dance floor, I felt gorgeous. Everybody watched us as we laughed and had fun. Dwight Eubanks, a long-time friend who was also my hair stylist, and quite flamboyant himself, danced near us and flirted with me. "Darling," he shouted, "You look delicious." Everybody laughed uncontrollably, including Rick and me, as Dwight danced all around us and on into the crowd, still flirting.

It was after three in the morning when Rick and I finally snuggled up in bed together. It had been a very long and exuberant day and I should have been exhausted, but I wasn't. In fact, I was still full of energy and wanted to talk.

"Didn't Jade and Taylor enjoy themselves tonight," Rick laughed.

"They really did. I don't think they sat down all night, especially Jade. I believe she danced with everybody."

"I'm glad we decided to let them be a part of our celebration, aren't you?" Rick asked.

"Of course, I'm glad. It wouldn't have been the same without them."

"Do you remember when you were this pregnant with Jade and Taylor?" Rick asked me, rubbing my stomach.

"What do you mean do I remember? How could I forget?"

The first seven years of our marriage had been like a fairytale. We were madly in love, and wonderfully blessed with careers that were exactly what we had always wanted to do.

Rick and I met in college, and we both had big dreams. We had worked hard and our goals had become a reality.

My husband had been drafted by the Golden State Warriors to play professional basketball in the NBA.

As a young teenager I had spent many hours fantasizing and dreaming about becoming a fashion model. After college, I realized my childhood dreams: I became an international fashion model and traveled around Europe, New York, San Francisco and Atlanta. Rick and I were married in San Francisco, and loved everything about our new city.

After two years with the Golden State Warriors Rick was traded to The Atlanta Hawks and after five years in the NBA, he was offered a contract with a team in Brescia, Italy, an hour from Milan. I had already spent quality time in Milan working there and loved it; so when Rick was given the opportunity to experience an international lifestyle, I encouraged him to take it and told him he could always go back to the NBA. He did.

Our lifestyle was glamorous and romantic in Italy, and at the end of our first year there together we decided to have our first child. I continued to work until I was five and a half months pregnant. I didn't tell my agent because I loved what I was doing and didn't want any problems, but how long can you keep a pregnancy concealed?

Tiziana was the owner and head booker for the fashion division at Why Not Models. I had worked with her agency from the very beginning of my Italian experience. I thought she would be happy for me, but I was mistaken.

As a matter of fact, when I told her, she hissed, "Darling, all of this work for nothing?" She shuffled papers on her desk, adding, "Well, I guess *love* is more important than work."

I was hurt and appalled that she could think otherwise. "Oh, don't worry, Tiziana" I said, "I'll work again after the baby is six months old."

"We'll see, Darling."

A few days later I received a phone call from her; she wanted me to take a train to Torino for a two-day booking for fashion shows.

"I'm showing, Tiziana."

"I told them, Darling. They don't care, they want *you*." I could hear in her voice that she was smiling. Everything about being pregnant and having our baby was totally amazing. My Italian doctors seemed just as excited as we were. They were more curious about our baby's gender than we were as well, and each time I went in for an examination they pulled out their little machine to do a sonogram. Ironically though, the baby wouldn't let them see between its legs; it kicked very energetically every time.

I had intended to have the baby in Italy, but I began to panic during the beginning of the eighth month of my pregnancy. "What if something goes wrong and I don't remember any of my Italian?" I'd ask Rick. He could never completely answer the question for me. After the basketball season ended, we took a flight back to Atlanta. Our baby was born in June, 1986. Rick and I were filled with joy, and we were totally surprised and in awe when the doctor announced, "It's a girl!" We named her Jade.

Everything had been unfolding just as we had planned. After Jade's six-week examination, the three of us took a flight back to Italy. We picked up where we had left off, just as I had promised Tiziana. When Jade was about six months old, she and I began traveling around Europe. Once again I hit the catwalk, strutting down long runways for top designers. It was fabulous!

***

It was the last night of the Italian 1988 Prêt-à-Porter (Ready to Wear) Spring Collection. The last show of the season had been for Georgio Armani. According to Tiziana, it had been a huge success. She invited all of her models out to a dinner party to celebrate the success of the season. We had made lots of money for Tiziana and her partner, and also for ourselves. They wanted to thank us.

When LuCelaina Sierra and I walked into the restaurant there must have been twenty beautiful models already sitting at the long table. The table was laden with exotic flowers and Italian champagne. Lu and I walked around the table giving everyone kisses on both cheeks. Just as we had seated ourselves comfortably, an elegant waiter poured champagne into my glass.

Tiziana and Vittorio, her partner, walked into the restaurant with huge smiles on their faces. Paulette, one of Tiziana's favorite girls leaned toward me, whispering, "They just finished counting the money." We all stood up and applauded Tiziana.

Dinner was lovely, and of course we were all having a wonderful evening talking about fashion, designers, models and everything that goes along with Fashion Week, and who was going on to Paris for the Collections there. The conversations were invigorating, but near the end of the dinner, without warning, I was overcome by an overwhelming feeling of sadness. *What is this?* I needed to know. Several minutes passed. Then it hit me! I knew what was happening. My heart was heavy, but at least I knew why I had that foreboding feeling. Now it was my turn to lean toward Paulette and whisper into her ear. "This is my last Collection," I said, grieved by reality.

"Don't say that, Chloé! What are you talking about?" Her brows knit together as she waited for my response. I believe she knew what I was contemplating. I didn't share my feelings or the revelation with anyone else that night. Instead, knowing the truth, I made the most of my last night as an international fashion model in Milan, Italy.

I've had seven wonderful years in the fashion industry, I tried to console myself. *Now it's over.* Rick and I had decided we wanted another baby, and I had to choose between being a committed, full-time mom or committing to my career. *Having more children is more important than my career. Isn't it?*

I had always been torn between my career and my family because of the traveling, even when it was just Rick and me. I knew one day it would come down to this. But the timing was off. Why now? It hit me like a ton of bricks coming out of nowhere. This was my reality and I had to accept it.

Rick had just recently signed a two-year deal for a team in Málaga, Spain. Jade and I joined him in November just a few weeks after my return from Italy. I loved Málaga— *La Costa del Sol*, they called it—but my heart longed for America, Atlanta in particular. I convinced my husband I needed to go home because Jade and I could commute from America to Spain every six weeks. He allowed me to have my way.

After returning to America with Jade I felt undervalued. I missed Milan and the excitement of my career and the job that I loved. Jade and I returned to Málaga in December for Christmas. We had a great time and it was wonderful during the holidays. Decorating the apartment and shopping for presents and gifts was so much fun. We were delighted we were together. After the holidays were over I had nothing productive to focus on. I didn't have anything to accomplish. So Jade and I packed up and flew back to Atlanta.

***

It was a very brisk, but sunny day at the end of January. It occurred to me that I was probably pregnant. Rick and I were ecstatic. We wanted a boy and planned to name him Taylor. Now I had something extremely positive to focus on, something to take my mind off the career I had sacrificed. I didn't feel as though I would be sitting around wasting my life. I had a strong desire to have another baby. *After all, this is why I gave up my career in the first place.*

Taylor made his debut on August fourth, three weeks earlier than he was supposed to arrive. I barely had time to make it to the delivery room. "I'm supposed to have an epidural," I moaned to the nurses as they rushed me into labor and delivery.

"Honey, it's not gon' do you a bit o' good." One of the nurses laughed.

"But I'm supposed to have it!" I cried louder.

"Well, we can give it to you, but before it even starts to work that baby's gon' be here."

They were right. Taylor was born thirty minutes after Rick and I walked into the hospital. He came out screaming and peeing all over the doctor.

"He looks just like me!" Rick shouted. We were filled with so much joy we cried.

***

The morning after our tenth anniversary and the big party, the pitter-patter of four little feet, running in the direction of our bedroom, awakened us. I felt drained and tired, as though I hadn't slept at all. "What time is it?" I rolled over, asking Rick.

"Seven forty-five."

"What? Seven forty-five?"

By now Jade and Taylor were jumping up onto our bed. They both had huge grins plastered across their faces. They wanted to talk about all the fun they'd had at our anniversary party.

"No!" I moaned. "Please guys, I'm still sleepy. I can't talk now."

"Yeah, I guess you can't talk. You didn't fall asleep until after four this morning." Rick laughed. He was in a better mood than me.

"Mommy can't talk now because she talked about you two all night long, and that's why she didn't fall asleep until after four o'clock," Rick told them.

"Why did you talk about us, Mommy?" Jade wanted to know.

"Mommy was reminiscing about you and Taylor being born."

"What's *reminiscing*?" They asked.

"I want to hear about us being born," Taylor whined.

"Oh no!" I cried, "I can't go through all of that again right now. I'll tell you guys tomorrow, okay?"

***

Justin, our third child, was born two months later; it was October seventeenth. Rick was in Madrid at the time.

"You can leave on the next flight after your wife calls saying your baby is here," the president of his basketball team had promised.

Having a baby without Rick right beside me made me nervous, even though it was my third delivery. Normie, my youngest sister, had been staying with me. She was my coach.

"Push! Push!" The doctor insisted. "I see his head, we're almost there! Push!"

She placed Justin on my chest, the culmination of our nine-month spiritual bonding process continuing. Crying, I peered down my nose at him. "He looks so sweet," I said to no one in particular. I felt joy again, and then wondered if this same joy comes each time a child is born. My baby sister looked over at me, crying too. "I've never experienced anything so profound," she said, drying her tears with the back of her hand. The nurse took the baby from me. "We'll give him right back to you, mom. We just need to check him."

"Call Rick right now," I ordered my little sister. "Then call everybody else." Normie left the room to carry out my request. I was very careful not to take my eyes off my baby while the doctor and attendants performed their routine examination.

"He's perfect." The doctor bragged, as though she'd had something to do with it. She handed him back to me

I was exhausted, excited, and amazed by the miracle of my third child's birth. I was still alert and in a very good mood when one of my brothers and two other sisters arrived to see the baby and me.

With authority, my sister Brenda announced to the nurse, "I want to hold my nephew." The nurse placed Justin into Brenda's arms as she sat in the rocking chair. "He's the prettiest baby you've had, Chloé." Brenda said, while Cherrie, Normie, and Ed gathered around her, gazing down at the baby.

"Okay everybody, we need to get mom ready to go to her room." This was the cue for everyone to leave.

"Chloé, we'll bring Jade and Taylor tomorrow after school." Normie told me as they began to leave. Less than a minute after they'd gone, Rick phoned from Madrid. He was crying and yelling, telling me how happy he was we'd had another son. "Baby!" he spoke loudly. "I just got home from Barcelona! I just checked my messages and heard Normie's voice telling me about the baby!" Rick's rapid speech was quick and punchy. I was extremely fatigued all of a sudden, and needed to leave the delivery room.

"Baby?" I pleaded.

"What is it?" Rick asked quickly.

"I'll have to call you back when I get to my room."

"Okay, I love you. Call me back in an hour!"

"Alright, I will." I was so tired, I didn't quite keep my promise.

Justin was absolutely beautiful, he weighed seven pounds and two ounces, and he was nineteen inches long. He had big feet and big ankles, like his father's side of the family. Jade and Taylor had been born with a head full of black curly hair; Justin had no hair on the side of his little head and just a little bit on top, and it was completely straight. I fell asleep with a peaceful smile on my face.

Early the next morning I called for my baby. I couldn't wait to hold him again. A nurse with a wide grin on her face rolled him into my room. My arms were stretched out to receive him before she reached the bed. She lifted him out of the little glass crib and placed him into my arms. Contented, I buried my nose in his neck. "You smell so good, and you're so cute, too." The nurse smiled as she took my vitals.

"It's Mommy. It's Mommy, Justin. I love you. Daddy's coming to see you soon." There was a brush in the crib. I asked the nurse to pass it to me. As I brushed Justin's hair, he made little cooing sounds. The whole miracle of this little baby in my arms made me cry. The nurse continued her work and smiled at the sight of us. Even though she'd surely seen this same picture a thousand times, I could tell she still loved to watch.

"You know all of this little hair is going to fall out, don't you?"

"Excuse me?" I was caught off guard by her remark.

"All of this is just temporary hair," she laughed. "It's going to fall out."

"No, I don't know that." I responded, annoyed by her comment. She laughed as though I didn't know a thing about babies.

"This is my *third child*," I made sure to let her know. "My older babies didn't lose any hair. As a matter of fact, my oldest son grew a large afro before his first birthday."

She smiled, changing the subject. "You can go ahead and kiss the baby. I need to take him for some tests and to have his first pictures taken." She took Justin out of my arms and placed him back into the little glass bed.

"Get some rest while you can." She rolled the baby out of the room. On her way out, peering down at Justin, she cooed, "You sure are a cute one, aren't you?"

After breakfast I fell asleep and slept for almost two hours without anyone bothering me. Suddenly fully awake and alert, I thought of my husband, but not for long. It was time to nurse the baby again. A different nurse brought Justin in this time. After giving me the baby, she sat at the foot of the bed, smiling as though she were my friend. She waited until Justin was positioned just right in my arms and nursing. Then she said gently, "Your baby has a heart murmur."

I looked up from the baby and studied the nurse's expression. She was calm, still smiling. "I found it," she said, still smiling. Before I could gather my thoughts and respond to what she had just told me, she added, "He also has jaundice. Your pediatrician will come by today to visit the baby. He'll talk to you after the examination."

Dr. Burnham walked in smiling. "Congratulations! I've just left your baby boy. He's cute."

"Thank you," I smiled back at him.

"He's going to be big, isn't he?"

"He's much bigger than Jade and Taylor were, that's for sure," I laughed.

After the usual pleasantries, the doctor mentioned Justin had jaundice. "This is not uncommon," he assured me. "It's nothing for you to worry about." Before I could exhale a sigh of relief, he handed me a piece of paper he had been writing on during our conversation.

"This is the name of a cardiologist. I want you to call him when you get home to make an appointment regarding the baby's heart murmur." Dr. Burnham continued. "He's one of the best pediatric cardiologists in the south."

CHAPTER 3
Baby Boy

Rick phoned the next morning. It was such a relief to hear his voice. He made me feel stronger. I told him what the pediatrician had said about the jaundice, the heart murmur, and taking the baby to see a cardiologist.

"Don't worry, love," he reminded me, "You have a heart murmur yourself, and you're fine. Our baby boy will be fine, too."

"You're right." I was encouraged. "I feel better already. I can't wait for you to get here." When Rick paused, I knew something wasn't right.

"What's wrong?"

"I can't come home for three more weeks. We have some tough games coming up, and they don't want me to leave."

Thinking of all the things I would have to do alone, I cried.

The baby and I remained in the hospital for seven days, which was longer than the routine stay. The next morning, after taking my vitals, the nurse finally told me I could check out.

"Great!" I beamed. "I just need to call my sister. What time should she pick us up?" The nurse spun around and looked me right in the eye.

"Oh! You can go ahead and check out now, but your baby's going to stay here for a few more days."

"Excuse me? What are you talking about?"

"The baby's jaundice is out of control; he needs to stay under the blue lights for at least two to three more days." I was shocked to hear my baby wasn't going home with me. I was insulted by the impersonal manner in which the nurse gave me this news. Her words were very detached when she said, "We'll do a bilirubin test every day and—"

"What's that?" My voice cracked as I cut her off. My hands covered my mouth. I started blinking rapidly, a nervous habit. *I can't just walk out of this hospital leaving my baby behind.* She interrupted my thoughts.

"A bilirubin test is a blood test done on newborn babies to test for jaundice. He'll be just fine, and you can take him home in a few days."

While she spoke I made up my mind. "I'm not going home without him."

"What's that, Hon?"

"I'm not going home without my baby. I'm staying right here until he's ready to go with me." She gawked at me kind of cock-eyed, hemming and hawing, telling me how much it was going to cost me because my insurance wouldn't pay. She said they needed the bed. I didn't care. I just knew I would not leave the hospital without my baby.

***

Three weeks later, Rick called to tell me he was coming home. "Don't tell Jade and Taylor. I want to surprise them." After arriving at the airport late in the afternoon, Rick took a taxi home and rang the doorbell.

"Now who could that be?" I asked the kids, sounding annoyed, but knowing very well who it was.

"Jade, would you please answer the door for Mommy?" I knew Taylor would follow her. I tiptoed several steps behind them. Just before they approached the door, Rick used his key and walked right inside. The kids went wild, screaming and yelling. They seemed almost afraid, not believing their eyes. They didn't know if they should laugh or cry. They were totally out of control. Tears welled up as I watched them.

After hugging, kissing, and tickling the kids, Rick finally saw me. He walked through the foyer and into the family room. Jade and Taylor were still holding onto his legs. I had been standing behind a large palm tree with the baby. When he reached us, he wrapped his arms around both of us. I was nervous his strong embrace might hurt the baby, so I pulled away a little bit. He held my face gently with both hands as he kissed me softly.

"I'm so happy to finally be home," he smiled. His eyes moved down to my arms where I cradled our baby. Rick took Justin very gently. He brought him up to his face. The baby was very small in Rick's large hands.

"Hello, baby boy," he whispered. "Daddy's home." I could tell by my husband's expression he was enchanted by his new son, just as much as he'd been when he first held Jade and Taylor.

CHAPTER 4

He's a Fighter

We held our breath as the doctor walked over to us. I didn't take my eyes off him. He motioned for us to sit down, pulling out a chair for me.

"Justin is alive," he said calmly. "When you brought him in this afternoon, there were no vital signs at all. We had to resuscitate him twice." He looked at us compassionately. "Who found him?"

Brenda was sitting where Rick and I had left her and Taylor, but when the doctor began speaking, I noticed her getting up, going over to Justin's bed. I could see her out of the corner of my eye.

The doctor noticed I had been distracted. He paused, then asked again. "Who found him?"

"I did."

"How long do you think he was in the water?" I started to backtrack in my mind. I remembered seeing Justin walking through the kitchen carrying his bag of French fries. I had been on the phone talking to Lena. *Lena!* I recalled with rage. *I hadn't wanted to talk on the phone anyway. Why did I answer it? Why did she have to call me so many times? She*

25

had called twice and left messages. She should have known if I wanted to talk to her I would have called her back. I was going to call her back. Why couldn't she just wait for me to call her back?

I tried to remember how long I had been on the phone. "It wasn't long." I started to say the same thing I had already said, trying to paint a clearer picture in my head. I saw Taylor and Justin watching TV, then they went outside; but they both came right back in, going to the library with Rick. Then I remembered Justin walking through the kitchen carrying his bag of French fries.

Frustrated and disappointed, I yelled, "I don't know how long Justin was in the pool! I didn't even know he was missing. But it couldn't have been a long time."

The doctor was patient. "Was it two, three, five, or ten minutes?" I started to think back quickly to what I remembered and guessed, "About five minutes."

Not until that moment did I realize a minute could make the difference between life and death. The doctor went on to tell us Justin was breathing, but he was connected to life support.

"We gave your son a medication which paralyzes him. We don't want him to move right now." We won't know anything for seventy-two hours, until after the medication wears off." The doctor asked, "Do you have any other children you need to go take care of? Anything you need to do?"

Brenda had taken Taylor to the waiting room so we could speak to the doctor. Our friend Joe had found Jade with friends at the mall, and brought her straight to the hospital. Now Rick and I headed home with Jade, Taylor, and Brenda.

Jade was devastated, thinking if she had been home, Justin would have been with her. I tried to reassure her none of this was her fault. I wanted to sit down with her to make sure she understood, but I couldn't. I needed to get back to Justin. I took off the scrubs, grabbed some things for Jade and Taylor, and got a toothbrush for myself. We then headed to Brenda's house, dropping her and the children off before going straight back to the hospital.

Rick and I cried all night in the ICU waiting room. There were lots of other families in the small waiting room, crying for their babies, too. Some had been there for days; others had been there for weeks; yet another had been there for two months. Babies and young children were critically ill, and dying.

Rick and I took turns going in to see Justin throughout the night. At 6:30 the next morning, both of us were back in Justin's room, waiting for any news about his condition.

By now there was a team of doctors working on Justin: a neurologist, a cardiologist, and a pediatric kidney specialist. I knew all of them already. Dr. Sherwinter, the pediatric kidney specialist, knew all of our children. He and his partner, Dr. Burnham, were their pediatricians. The neurologist was the same doctor who had diagnosed Justin with hypotonia at nine months, and had seen him on a regular basis since then. The cardiologist had diagnosed Justin with a ventricular septal defect two weeks after his birth.

Justin had been a fighter since the very beginning. He was tough. After two years of medication for the ventricular septal defect, the hole in his heart finally closed. "Justin can now be considered a normal, healthy, husky baby boy," his doctor had declared. We'd laughed joyously because our supposedly sickly son was sweetly plump, and we thanked God for our son's health. *Praise the Lord*!

The doctors were all very hopeful. We could see the compassion in their faces, especially in Dr. Sherwinter's. Nevertheless, they had to let us know the seriousness of Justin's condition. His neurologist explained to us a "near drowning" experience such as Justin's and the loss of oxygen to the brain was very serious. Justin's cardiologist was preparing to test his heart, and would have the results in a few hours. Dr. Sherwinter explained Justin would need kidney dialysis. He told us we should continue to pray and hope for the best.

Chapter 5
Special

At 6'9" and 250 pounds, Rick had been a competitive athlete for most of his life. My husband was accustomed to taking action. He wanted to *do something* to move this situation along smoothly, and make it turn out favorable for his family. *But what*—he was asking himself repeatedly, almost begging—*What can I do?*

Watching my husband's helplessness prompted me to review my own feelings of inadequacy and guilt about what had happened.

"I actually found my baby floating in the pool?" I cried softly, still in shock. I wasn't really speaking to anyone in particular, but talking to anyone who would listen. The doctors and the nurse paused looking at me compassionately without saying anything.

***

I reflected on having the pool built in the first place, and wanted desperately to find some fault with myself for not talking my husband out of it. But the kids and I had been ecstatic when Rick phoned from Madrid three years earlier. He had been so energized, so upbeat. Usually he is very laid-back and never overly excited about anything, but this day was different. "Go ahead," he said boldly, "and design the pool."

"Really?" I asked, excited, and somewhat shocked. We had not spoken about putting in a pool for a while, and now, all of a sudden the subject seemed to come up out of nowhere.

"Have it built, too!" he said. I could tell in his excitement he felt good about his decision. Jade and Taylor had wanted their own pool for a while now, so out they came with shrieks of happiness.

Rick told me he wanted the pool finished by the time basketball season was over. At the time, I'd been more than happy to accommodate him. It was something *the whole family* wanted.

Our entire backyard was soon gutted and transformed into a tropical oasis. I supervised everything, down to each flower, plant, and tree. When Rick got home, and saw what I had designed, he was thoroughly impressed.

Rick and the children lived at the poolside. They were busy and content the entire summer. Jade and Taylor swam like fish, and never wanted to get out of the water. They weren't satisfied though until I allowed Justin, who was only nine months old at the time, to float with them. He loved it.

One late afternoon Rick and the children were down in the pool with our neighbor's three children. They splashed, raced, jumped from the waterfall, and played ball. When I tried to get them to come up to eat, they refused. Even Rick said he wasn't hungry. He absolutely loved being with the children—I believe as much as they loved being with him. I knew they needed to eat so I made little sandwiches, lemonade, and sliced some fruit up, and took it down to the pool and placed it on one of the tables. Each kid climbed out of the water one by one, picked up a sandwich, ate it quickly, gulped down a glass of lemonade and jumped right back into the water. *Well, I'm doing the best I can here*, I laughed to myself. *If they want more at least they'll know it's not too far from the pool.*

I had been upstairs for about half an hour when I heard the children in some kind of commotion. Jade was the loudest. What's that?" I heard the children asking.

"Daddy, Daddy!"

"Mr. Brown, Mr. Brown! Look! Look what's in the pool!"

I looked out of the window and saw the kids racing out, leaving Justin on his float, and Rick in the water beside him. Jade raced up the steps to the kitchen. "Mommy, Mommy! Guess what! There's poop in the pool. Justin pooped in the pool!"

The matter was undeniably one which needed to be taken care of right away. However, all I could do was stand there and laugh at her disgusted expression, which told the story of the major catastrophe. The faces of her friends told the same story. They stood behind her, shaking their heads in agreement.

Taylor was the last child to come in. "Mommy," he whined, "I don't want to swim *no* more!"

At this point my laughter was out of control. I couldn't help myself. I took advantage of the situation. "So! This is what it takes to get you guys out of the pool for a while!"

They didn't have time to respond before Rick walked in the back door with the baby. He walked over and handed him to me and walked back down to the pool to clean up the mess.

Justin had always had a love affair with water from the very beginning. He loved bath time too, never wanting to come out of it. Whenever he was with us at the pool he never cried or complained about anything. I bought him little orange sunglasses. He looked like a baby movie star lounging on his float, wearing only his birthday suit and sunglasses.

***

When Justin was about three months old, I noticed he wasn't doing the same kinds of things Jade and Taylor had done at that age. I mentioned this to his pediatrician right away.

"It's not uncommon for babies born with a serious heart defect, such as Justin's, to develop a little bit slower. Don't worry, he'll catch up," he assured me.

I had been following a little booklet about what babies were supposed to be doing at certain ages and stages. I got frustrated and threw the booklet in the trash when Justin was four months old. My son wasn't catching up.

When I mentioned my concerns to family members, they all told me it wasn't fair to compare Justin to Jade and Taylor. I felt guilty and stopped for a couple of months, but at Justin's six-month check-up I brought up my concerns to the pediatrician again. He repeated the same thing. "It's because of the heart defect." For the next three months, I watched Justin very closely. I knew I had to put my foot down, so when I took my son in for his nine-month check-up I insisted we see a neurologist.

"Here's the name and number of a wonderful group of neurologists at Scottish Rite Children's Hospital. I've worked with them quite a bit." The pediatrician was finally listening to me.

***

We filled out all of the necessary forms and answered the questions as best we could. Now we waited for the doctor. After fifteen minutes, Dr. Goldstein walked into the room with a smile on his face, extending his hand to me, and then to Rick, as he introduced himself. He was young and fairly handsome, wearing wire-framed glasses, a Polo shirt, and baggy pants that needed ironing. He walked over to the table where I held the baby. He lifted Justin up with both his hands under the baby's armpits. Justin slipped right through. He did this again, and once more—the same thing happened. "Okay." The doctor said to himself, "I see."

He continued, tickling the baby. Justin laughed loudly. The doctor noticed right away Justin was very personable. "You're cute," he said, tickling him again. Turning toward us, he asked, "Does he mimic you? Repeat words or sounds?" Rick and I looked at each other. "Yes," we both agreed, "he repeats a few sounds. His favorite is *dada*, of course."

As soon as *dada* came out of my mouth, Justin repeated it.

"Dada," he babbled. The doctor laughed. Rick and I smiled to each other.

"It appears to me Justin has a muscle disorder called hypotonia," the doctor told us. He explained briefly what hypotonia entails. "He probably won't walk before he's eighteen months old. We need to get him into physical therapy right away."

I was devastated by these words. I cried and cried. I heard Rick say, as he put his arms around me, "Uh, uh, uh." He held me while Dr. Goldstein held Justin.

"I know this is difficult, but it's not as bad as it appears," the doctor said, interrupting my sobbing. "I've seen amazing improvements after therapy. Justin seems to be a pretty determined little guy. The best thing is, we've detected it early." As hard as this news was for me to hear, I liked this doctor's attitude.

"All along I knew something wasn't right," I told the young neurologist. "But nobody listened to me."

"*Sometimes mothers know more than anyone else,*" Dr. Goldstein admitted. "I'm going to write a prescription right now for therapy to begin immediately." He handed Rick a piece of paper. "Take this down to the third floor. Make an appointment to start therapy right away. When you get to the front desk, make an appointment to bring Justin back in three weeks."

I realized then and there I needed to change my attitude quickly. I needed to become proactive.

We reached the third floor where all the physical therapists were working. We were informed there had been a cancellation. "You can start right now if you like," the young lady scheduling the appointments said. She leaned in and whispered, "This therapist is the best." Rick and I both agreed this was a blessing, and we accepted.

We were escorted right into a large room where several therapists were working with their patients. We watched everything Justin's therapist did. She wanted us to do the same thing at home. Justin liked her, because he enjoyed the games they played.

During the next three weeks, Justin went to physical therapy three times a week. He made tremendous improvements. It seemed almost miraculous. Jade and Taylor liked working with Justin, too.

I asked his therapist if it was all right for Justin to continue to play in the pool. "That's wonderful exercise, if he likes being in the water," she said. So, for Justin, things went along rather naturally. Therapy was working! *Praise the Lord.*

To me Justin was the sweetest, cutest baby I'd ever seen in real life. His lips were extremely kissable, just like the Gerber baby. Jade and Taylor adored their baby brother and they were very protective. They knew how special he was, and about all the doctors Justin had seen. During all of this, my baby continued to take the medication for his heart defect twice a day. But Justin never complained; he was a tough cookie.

Amazingly, he never cried when he got his immunization shots. "Does he have a high tolerance for pain?" I asked the pediatrician, Dr. Burnham.

"I suppose so," he said. "Some babies are just tougher than others."

I reminded him of Jade and Taylor's high-pitched screams whenever they'd gotten their injections. He rubbed his lip and cocked his head to one side, reflecting.

"Oh yes," he recalled. "Taylor cried long after an injection once, all the way into the reception room and out the door. I came back into the room after the nurse left to make sure everything was okay." I was impressed Dr. Burnham had actually remembered. He and I laughed together while Justin blew him a kiss good-bye.

CHAPTER 6
Pulling Through

After everything Justin had been through so far, I knew *God wasn't going to let him die.* I had been a good person, a wonderful mother and wife, and a dear friend. Surely I hadn't done anything to deserve a punishment so severe. God just *couldn't* let my baby die.

This is a test. I'll pass it, I told myself, even though I was seriously frightened by everything going on around me. Rick and I were faced with a major crisis. *No matter what, I will continue to be upbeat and positive.* I had to, for my family and for myself.

At ten o'clock the next morning, Dr. Burnham came to Justin's bedside with tears in his eyes as he told us how sorry he was. He looked down at Justin and caressed his hand. He didn't speak very much. His body language said he wanted to do something, but just as Rick had felt helpless earlier, now it was the doctor who felt helpless. It was out of his hands. I knew Dr. Burnham wanted to take control, to tell us how things would get better. But he could not. Still, Rick and I were comforted by his presence.

"If the two of you need me, please call," he insisted, as he wiped away tears.

While the cardiologist ran all the necessary tests, Rick and I went back to the waiting room to find some coffee. It was so crowded we stood out in the hallway to drink our coffee. As I paced up and down, I saw Dr. Van Orden. She was Jade's pediatrician. Dr. Van Orden approached us with tears running down her face. She was definitely not her normal, composed self. She spoke rapidly, and I could feel her petite body shaking as she hugged me. She hugged Rick, too. "Please don't hesitate to call if you need me." She covered her face with her hands, and walked out.

After seeing two of our pediatricians so upset, I worried even more, and became more afraid. I was intent on remaining calm and positive until Justin's medication wore off. I imagined Rick and I would be sitting at his bedside, and he would slowly wake up, turn toward us, and wonder, "Where am I?" Then he would see me and reach for me to pick him up. I would be there for him. That's what I believed would happen.

For the last sixty hours, it seemed that everyone we knew, all across America, had prayed for Justin and for us. Hundreds of phone calls and messages arrived for us in the waiting room. We were even allowed to have phone calls next to Justin's bed.

When Lena found out what had happened, she rushed to the hospital. In tears, she encouraged me to be strong. In her thick accent she tried to encourage me. "Chloé," she began, looking me directly in the eye as she held my hands. "Now, Girl, you know where your strengths gon' have to come from, and I ain't talkin' about nothin' you get from yourself. I'm talkin' about the strength from our Father, Girl. You hear me, Chloé?"

Lena had been one of the first people I met when I moved to San Francisco years ago. She had always talked about God and her Father, so I knew exactly which Father she meant. She sat by Justin's bed for almost two hours praying for him. Then, after leaving his bedside, she went to the chapel to pray. I wasn't mad at Lena anymore. Just as I had told Jade, it was nobody's fault.

***

Justin was almost two years old when I began to have feelings of uncertainty about my life. I was a so-called *New Woman*. I needed something exciting to do again, something to accomplish, just for me. Rick had always been extremely supportive—he would give me the moon, if it were up for sale—but this had nothing to do with him. The more I tried to keep myself busy with Jade and Taylor's school and other activities involving the kids, the more undervalued I felt, like many stay-at-home mothers. I knew I was a great wife and an awesome mother. *But what about me?*

Quite a few years had passed since I had thought of my great-grandmother, Momma Freddie. When I heard myself asking *What about me?*, her words of wisdom came back very clearly.

Before Rick and I were married he had to be approved by Momma Freddie, the matriarch of the family. She was in her late eighties and had lost most of her vision, but her mind was still sharp and clear. After a long conversation with Rick and me, she gave her approval. "Son, you seem like a real nice boy. I believe you'll do the right thing."

Rick looked over at me, grinning sheepishly. "Yes ma'am," he assured Momma Freddie. "I'll do the right thing. I'll take good care of her." Both of us wanted to laugh at her, but we knew better.

Then, Momma Freddie wanted to talk to me. "Alone," she said. Rick walked outside. Momma Freddie waited until she heard the screen door slam shut before she began. "Baby, he seems like a real nice young man. He speaks so soft." She hesitated, gathering her thoughts, and then she continued. "Child, no matter how much money your husband may have, you always need to have your own." I was shocked. What she said seemed to come out of nowhere. Momma Freddie continued, "When I married Wiley, I had my own. I had my own land. Hundreds of acres," she boasted. "My own cows and mules, hogs and chickens, and everythang. Of course now, when I married Wiley, we came together and did thangs together and respected each other. But I still always maintained my own affairs." She questioned me directly. "You understand what I'm trying to tell you, Child?"

"Yes ma'am, I understand."

When I was a little girl I loved watching my great-grandmomma Freddie conduct her business. She was the boss lady when it came to her *affairs,* as she called it. Nonetheless, I heard people gossiping sometimes behind her back; but most people had nothing but great respect for her.

That's it! *That's exactly what I want*: RESPECT. I decided right then and there I would go back to work as a model—at least until I could figure out what I really wanted to do with my life. I had always enjoyed modeling, and hindsight is crystal clear. I admitted to myself I had given up my career prematurely. I knew international modeling was out for me. It was far behind me. *But that's okay. I'll try local modeling again.*

The very next day, I called L'Agence Models, an agency I had worked with when Rick was traded to the Atlanta Hawks, long before we had children. "When do you guys have open calls for new models?" I asked the lady on the other end of the phone.

"Every Wednesday afternoon from three to five," she told me routinely. She had certainly answered the question a hundred times already that day.

I waited two weeks, put on the coolest outfit I had in my closet, and showed up for the open call. While getting dressed and putting on my make-up, I felt confident. I knew this was something I could do well. Yet, when I walked into the agency and looked around, even though everything was familiar, I suddenly felt totally out of place. I could have been the mother of some of the young girls sitting there, waiting for their once-in-a-lifetime opportunity. I felt as though I was making a fool of myself, and decided to leave.

Just as I was about to make my escape, my friend Mark recognized me. "Chloé!" Mark called my name in total surprise. "What are you doing here?" He didn't wait for me to respond before he grabbed me and kissed me on each cheek.

"I want to be a model," I admitted to him, feeling quite silly at this point.

"What? You already are," he insisted, and went on to ask me about Rick and Jade. I told him that Rick was doing great, still playing basketball in Europe.

"You wouldn't recognize Jade now. She's in the second grade."

"You're kidding," he laughed. "That was quick." Mark asked me a few more questions about Jade, and then it dawned on me that he didn't know I had two sons. How would he have known? I had been out of touch for so many years. "Mark, did you know I have two boys? They're almost five and two."

Mark's jaw fell. "You're lying, right?"

Laughing nervously, I repeated their ages. "No, Taylor will be five in a few weeks, and Justin is almost two." He obviously hadn't heard me the first time I said it.

"Darling!" Mark screamed in disbelief. "I can't believe you've got three kids! You look *fabulous*! And you're serious about coming back to work too, aren't you?"

"Yes I'm serious," I laughed, still feeling nervous. *Who am I kidding?* I was married with three children *and* thirty-five years old. I waited for Mark's response.

"Perfect timing, Darling." His face lit up. "We've just hired a fabulous lady to head up our runway division. She's going to love you. "Wait here. I'll be right back." Mark left, but returned very quickly with a young, tall, elegant brunette. She appeared to be about twenty-five.

"Chloé, this is Madeleine."

I was in. Just like that. I had returned to modeling once again.

So many times in our lives we aren't paying attention, so we miss the evidence of God right where we are. *This experience was a God moment.* Had Mark not seen me and called out to me, I would have given up on this part of my dream. But there he was, and he did see me. He confirmed

41

what God had for me at this time in my life: a return to what I loved to do.

***

I sat on Justin's bed holding his little hand. He was perfectly still. His face was puffy. I still knew he was going to be just fine because I had my faith and courage. "I know you're going to wake up Justin, and when you do, Mommy's going to be right here."

I walked over to the desk and picked up the phone. I needed to call Madeleine to tell her to cancel all of my bookings, indefinitely. I didn't know when I would work again. Madeleine was out of the country, so I left a message. Naturally, all of the people at L'Agence were heartbroken about what had happened. By now, everyone in the local fashion industry had heard the devastating news. They started pouring into the hospital two and three at a time.

Brenda had come back to the hospital with Jade and Taylor, along with my other brothers and sisters. Also, Janise, the children's godmother; Bobby Jo, my best friend from college; my cousins Vicki and Tafuma; Aunt Anita; and so many other people came to the hospital. *Justin had in one way or another made an impact on these people, and they all loved him.*

Rick and I took turns going in with each person to see Justin. For those who wanted to pray for him we showed them where the chapel was located. Each time I went to Justin's bedside with a family member or friend for the first time, they gasped in disbelief. There were so many tubes and wires. I felt as though I needed to console them and let them cry on my shoulder. I had to be strong for them. At the same time, I had to assure Jade and Taylor that Justin was going to be fine. They were so afraid for their little brother when they saw all the wires and tubes. But they had me. If Mommy said Justin was going to be fine, then he was going to be fine.

I knew in my heart Justin was going to pull through this horrifying experience. I just had to be patient. The next day and a half were filled with hope. I knew God was going to perform a miracle.

Finally, the third day came, the day the medication would be wearing off. I was filled with confidence Justin was going to wake up out of the induced coma. We sat by his bed all day. I wasn't discouraged at all when he didn't wake up right away. A slow wake-up from medication was not uncommon for him. I recalled how medication for a serious febrile seizure in the middle of the night had knocked Justin out for days. "Even after a week he wasn't his normal self," I said, trying to convince Lin, the nurse. She said nothing, but I saw compassion in her eyes.

***

At 12:30 in the morning I was awakened by little sounds on the intercom coming from Justin's room. He wasn't crying, but the noises he made were unusual. I went upstairs to check on him. I got to his room and he was still lying in his crib asleep. The sounds had stopped. As I stood there looking down at him a soft voice inside of me whispered, *Take him downstairs with you.*

Back in my room, I took his temperature again. It was a little high but I needed to wait at least an hour before I could give him another dose of Tylenol. I put Justin in my bed, snuggled up next to him and kissed his forehead. I fell asleep admiring his beauty. There is something so sweet and special about a sleeping baby.

Around 3:00 in the morning I was awakened by little kicks from Justin. I didn't understand what he was doing. I thought maybe he was dreaming, but the kicking didn't stop. I sat up in bed, turning on the lamp. "Justin," I called, lifting him into my arms. He did not respond. I noticed he was still sleeping, but he was making strange sounds. I became alarmed, jumping up with Justin in my arms in one leap. I called his name loudly several times.

Just as I reached the door to walk out of my bedroom, I realized my baby boy was having a seizure. Crying, I ran to the phone and called 911. They asked a few important questions and confirmed my fears, staying on the phone with me until the fire department arrived, which was in only two minutes. The operator then told me the paramedics would be there in approximately three minutes.

I opened the back door, letting in four firefighters. As I stepped back from the door, the short stocky one took Justin out of my arms without saying a word, laying him down on the sofa. Quickly, he put an oxygen mask over Justin's little face. A tall, heavy one, who seemed to be in charge, began asking me questions. He realized almost immediately he wasn't getting any answers. I was too distracted. I needed to watch what the others were doing to my baby.

"Who else is in the house?" he asked. Not until now did I realize I had two other children upstairs. They would need someone to stay with them. I thought of Cecelia, my neighbor next-door. I called and explained what I thought was going on, and asked if she could come. Then I called Brenda, telling her exactly what I had told Cecelia.

"I'll be right there," they both said. I slammed down the phone. By now the paramedics were banging on the door. One of the firemen opened it and told the paramedics what was going on. As soon as the paramedics entered, the firemen let them take over.

Less than five minutes after I phoned Cecelia, she walked through the back door, ready to do whatever I needed. I didn't have to tell her anything. She was a mother, too. She knew what to do. The paramedics ripped Justin's pajamas off, and rushed him outside into the cold November night air.

"Cover him up with his blanket," I demanded, running behind them with his favorite blankie.

"His fever is a hundred and four," shouted a paramedic who carried him to the ambulance.

I sat in the cab of the ambulance with the driver. We arrived at Scottish Rite Children's Hospital in just a few minutes. I followed the paramedics right into the emergency room, watching, as they frantically worked on Justin. I became extremely nervous when I saw how jumpy they were. I began asking questions. They tried to answer as they continued to work on him. But I wouldn't let up.

"Please, step outside for a while, Mrs. Brown," they requested. As tears welled up, I threw my head back so they wouldn't run down my cheeks. I reluctantly stepped out of the room.

I was determined to keep my composure. As I stepped forward, other hospital workers ran into the room where I had just left my baby. I paced up and down. I came across an empty room, and made a quick decision to go in. Falling down on my knees I began to pray. I prayed hard, with conviction, and I cried even harder. Bent over, with my face in my hands, I felt a warm, comforting hand on my shoulder.

"This looks like a good place to be." said a soft voice behind me. "May I join you?" I opened my eyes, turned, and looked up to see a delicate smile looking toward me. It was a middle-aged blonde woman, the chaplain on call that night.

"Yes, of course," I said, without asking any questions for the first time that night. She knelt down beside me, and as I prayed she held my hand. When I stopped, she took over, praying beautifully, giving me support and comfort.

Justin was finally stabilized, and taken to ICU. He had several needles in him with IVs connected, even one in his temple. The nurses told me he had been given strong doses of Phenobarbital and Dilantin to stop the seizure, so he probably wouldn't wake up until tomorrow afternoon.

Justin actually didn't wake up until the following morning after that, which really scared all of us. I sat by his bed the entire time, just watching him. We refused to leave his bedside, and sure enough, both of us were standing right there when he opened his eyes. At first, it seemed he couldn't see us. Then he inspected his surroundings a little more, stared at me, and held both arms out toward me. Brenda laughed and cried, "Justin knows his mommy."

I leaned over to lift him up, but just at that moment one of the nurses walked over and stopped me. "I need to examine him first," she said.

As the nurse examined him Brenda started making a smacking sound with her mouth. It was one of Justin's favorite sounds to mimic. Brenda made the sound several times, and then Justin repeated it. She did this again and Justin repeated her again. Hot tears flowed, down my face and onto my shirt collar. Brenda and I hugged each other tightly. Now, I knew my baby—our baby, *everybody's baby*—was going to be just fine.

After three days in the hospital, Justin came home.

***

Once again, Justin was in the hospital in critical condition. Pryor to this time he had on two other occasions experienced very serious medical problems and had to be hospitalized. This time, having been found floating in our family pool, his medical condition was much more serious. Justin's neurologist, Dr. Goldstein, told Rick and me that he wanted to talk with us in the conference room. I had always respected and liked him. Today, however, his demeanor was different. He was very direct, reiterating the seriousness of the situation. Then he paused, took in some air, and let it out slowly. "It's unlikely that Justin is going to come out of this. There has been a lot of damage to his brain. He lost too much oxygen to the brain, and there's nothing now that can restore his brain cells."

We looked at him blankly. He continued, "I know how important it is for you to continue to have hope. But at the same time, you need to think about his quality of life. If he does live, he will be in a vegetative state." He paused, looking us in the eye. "You may need to think about taking him off life support."

Why are you trying to make us give up hope? I wanted to ask, but I couldn't get the words out. They were stuck in my mind, not even reaching my throat.

Rick and I cried softly, holding hands under the table. My husband tried to compose himself to ask a question, but I couldn't understand what he was trying to ask, and neither could the doctor. Rick cried harder. I wiped my tears away and composed myself enough to beg, "But there is a *possibility* Justin could pull through this, isn't there?"

"Yes," the doctor replied, "there is always the possibility for a *miracle*, but it's not likely based on what I've seen—"

"Thank you," I cut him off. I was very upset now. I just wanted to get back to Justin's bedside. I certainly wasn't going to let him have the final word.

CHAPTER 7

Got Game Today

Jade and Taylor had missed the first two days of the new school year. All of their friends, and the entire school heard what had happened to Justin, so everyone was very concerned. Jade and Taylor had not seen many of their friends since May. When they walked into the building, a crowd of people showered them with hugs. It was a wonderful blessing that they had so much support at school.

My Aunt Anita had been taking care of the house and the children. Rick's mother had flown in from California, and Angela, Aunt Anita's daughter, had flown in from New York. Everyone wanted to console us in some way. I continued to be strong. I felt like I had no choice. I believed everyone in the family had been watching me, to gauge how they should respond. I had to keep my composure for everyone else. Every time someone asked how I was doing, I'd lie, "I'm fine."

Lin, Justin's nurse, couldn't take it any longer. She had been there since the first night, watching me comfort almost everyone who came to Justin's bedside. After seeing me frantically trying to calm one of my friends after an emotional outburst, she walked over to us.

"Mrs. Brown," she cried, grabbing my arm forcefully. "You're *not okay*! Stop trying to be strong for everybody else. Think about yourself!"

Lin was right. I tried to compose myself, but I failed miserably. My tears burst through like a ruptured dam. *She had given me permission to be human*. She held me, rubbed my back, and patted my head. Her embrace was strong and comforting. I wanted to stay there for as long as she would let me.

"I've watched you for three days console everybody who has come in here," she told me. "It's okay for you to cry and be weak. You can't be strong for everyone all the time. From now on, I'm letting only family in here. I know all of these people really love you and your husband, but it's wearing you down."

I was incredibly weak. I hadn't eaten in three days. I'd had only water and coffee. In three days I had become a chain smoker. Lin talked Rick into taking me home. I heard her tell him, "She needs to take a long bath. Try to get her to rest for a few hours before she comes back. And make her eat something."

But home wasn't exactly the place for finding rest. The phone never stopped ringing, the TV was blaring continuously, and people were constantly in and out.

Still, Aunt Anita and my mother-in-law were amazing. That night, my aunt made a wonderful dinner, piled a plate up high for me, and placed it in front of me as I sat at the kitchen counter.

"I want you to eat every bit of this," she demanded. I ate a few forks full, then moved the food around on my plate until she took it away.

Rick decided to go back to the hospital. He begged me to stay home with Jade and Taylor until he returned. I knew he would phone me as soon as he got there. I spent time with Jade and Taylor in their room until they fell asleep.

When I came downstairs, my mother-in-law was sitting on the deck alone. I decided to share my feelings with her. For the first time I broke down crying in front of a family member. I held my face in my hands. Over the muffled yells and squeals of pain pouring from me, I heard my mother-in-law whimper, "Chloé, don't you do this to me." Now, she too, was weeping uncontrollably. Like me, she had held it in as long as she could, trying to be strong for everyone else. We sobbed in each other's arms.

I fell asleep waiting for Rick. He had promised to come back for me.

***

"Chloé! Chloé! Chloé!" Several photographers called to me as bulbs flashed. I was on the runway in Milan, but everyone there was from Atlanta. All the photographers wanted me to look into their lenses, but I couldn't see. I was temporarily blinded.

"Mommy! Mommy! Mommy!" My children called in unison. They were all the same age: around three or four. "Look at me, Mommy! I want you, Mommy!" they all screamed.

"I can do it, too!" Jade boasted.

"No, let me do it!" Taylor whined.

"I want my mommy!" Justin cried at me, very clearly. I wanted to do something. But I was distracted and blinded by all the flashing lights.

"Mrs. Brown, this is the pediatrician's office. Justin has been progressing, but the fact remains that his development is definitely delayed. We need more aggressive treatment for Justin. We need to do a muscle biopsy."

"What's that?"

"Surgery. We have to cut some muscle from Justin's thigh."

"No! Don't cut my baby. He wants his blankie. Where is Justin's blankie? He just wants me!"

***

"Chloé, Chloé!" Rick called softly, waking me from my nightmare.

"Rick," I said, disoriented. "Where is Justin?" I was exhausted. The words barely escaped my parched lips. "What time is it?" Before Rick could answer, I remembered what was happening. "You promised you were coming back for me."

"You're too tired." He insisted, "you needed to rest. "I called, but your aunt said you were sleeping. We didn't want to wake you."

"How is Justin doing?" I begged, trying to get up.

"He was moving a little, and he tried to open his eyes."

At that news, I wanted desperately to go back to the hospital, but Rick pleaded with me to try to rest and wait until morning. There was something strange in Rick's voice. He should have been excited Justin had been moving, even if it was just a little. But he was exhausted, too. Both of us needed rest. Reluctantly, I gave in. My body felt like lead. I couldn't lift myself from the bed anyway. I cried myself back into a deep sleep.

***

We arrived at the hospital early the next morning. It was the fifth day. The doctors informed us that the medication had worn off completely. As we sat there looking at our sweet little Justin, he began to move and make sucking and smacking sounds with his mouth and lips. I was extremely encouraged and told the nurses, "Justin does that all the time, especially when he has his blanket." I put his blankie closer to his face. He had the habit of throwing his blankie around his neck like a scarf or shawl. I knew he would know it was there and it would make him feel better. It always did.

"What Justin is doing is called *reflexes*," a nurse told me. Lin was off duty that day. "They're the most basic reflexes. All lower animals do this."

Lower animals? What is she trying to say? I wept hysterically over her insensitive remarks, but I wasn't about to give up my faith that Justin would recover.

Rick and I, our families, and most of our friends stayed in the hospital chapel praying. Some of the guys who played basketball with (or against) Rick at one time or another came to the hospital to pray with us; so many others called. Several of the priests from Saint Jude were in and out of Justin's room a lot. Even preachers and pastors from other churches heard about Justin and asked their congregations to pray.

My Aunt Shirley and her husband, Napoleon, came. So many friends, and even people we didn't know, sent food and flowers. After some time had passed I realized with profound gratitude how wonderful and supportive our entire Atlanta community had been.

At Sunday mass exactly one week after the accident, Monsignor O'Conner explained to the parish what had happened to Justin. He also told them what we were going through. He asked everyone to pray for a miracle.

After mass we all went straight to the hospital to be with Justin. When we got there I saw that my Uncle Arvern, Aunt Anita's husband and my mother's older brother, had just arrived. Uncle Arvern, who had always been so strong, stood over Justin with his head bent and his tears fell onto the bed. He spoke incredibly softly but he was stern. "This is a tragedy! We need to do some *serious praying.*" He hugged me and then he hugged Rick, Taylor, and Jade. Moving very, very slowly, he sat down in the chair next to Justin's bed. We all cried.

Lin asked if I wanted to hold Justin.

"What about all the wires and tubes?" I asked.

"Sit down here and I'll give him to you."

I sat there patiently waiting for Lin to untangle wires and position the tubes so I could hold my baby. I sobbed and shook. Lin placed Justin in my arms for the first time in seven days. I was terribly frightened because he was so stiff. I couldn't snuggle close to him. He didn't melt into my arms the way he liked to do. He had no idea I was there.

The kids wanted to take Uncle Arvern to the chapel to show him around. They had become very familiar with the hospital. They left Rick and me alone with our baby boy.

I watched Justin struggle to open his eyes. Finally, I realized looking into his eyes was unbearable. His beautiful, almond-shaped, brown eyes had always had a twinkle in them. This day the whites of his eyes were bluish-gray and his pupils were bluish-black. They weren't Justin's eyes anymore.

I cried out from the center of my stomach, overcome by pain and fear. My heart and soul felt pierced by daggers. I couldn't breathe. I was being stabbed to death. Rick cried out, too. He couldn't be strong any longer. We held onto each other for strength. At that moment we knew Justin would never see us again.

As we walked out of ICU and into the waiting room, we decided not to say anything to anyone yet. Everyone was hungry. Jade and Taylor wanted to eat somewhere outside the hospital. We understood. They had been so patient. Rick and I had no idea what we were going to tell them about their baby brother.

As we walked out of the hospital a soft voice, just above a whisper, spoke to me: *Don't worry*, He said. *Justin's spirit left his body last Sunday.*

***

A mother's love for her babies is often intense and extremely intimate. Sometimes she feels what they feel and knows what they're thinking. This is how it was for me with each of my babies. However, there had been something much deeper between Justin and me. Sometimes when he was there beside me I felt as though he was trying to get back inside me. It felt like he couldn't get close enough. Maybe it was because he was a child of so few words. I really did know what he wanted almost all the time and I had always been right there for him.

55

***

After I'd made the decision to return to modeling, it had been difficult for Justin. Unlike Jade and Taylor, he was a year and a half old before he had a babysitter. Consequently, he didn't want to have anything to do with her. But Rick and I felt fortunate, even blessed, to find Cheryl. She was a strong, caring, and patient woman who had been a teacher for several years before becoming a nanny. She was just the kind of person we wanted to care for our children.

Justin didn't like Cheryl much when she arrived but he tolerated her because Jade and Taylor liked her a lot. Because Cheryl had been a teacher she knew how to work with Justin in many ways that I didn't. I was very impressed and thankful. Justin's old room had been turned into a classroom for him. There were lots of books, puzzles, manipulative objects for motor development, a tape recorder for Justin to speak into so he could hear his own voice, paints, crayons, and many other educational items. All of this was to help him to develop and learn while having fun.

We had a large closet upstairs in the hallway that wasn't being used. We turned it into an art center where the kids could write, draw, and paint on the wall. It turned out to be so much fun. Almost everyone who came to our house and saw the room wanted to autograph the wall or draw on it. It became a cool place to visit. Justin loved putting his signature on it just like everybody else.

There was a new special class opening for three- and four-year-olds at Jade and Taylor's school. Justin was accepted. We couldn't believe our luck. Two of the teachers came to our home to interview us and get to know Justin before he began his classes. We were very impressed with Mrs. Neu, his personal teacher. We liked her right away.

Rick or I would take all the children to school together each morning. Justin was so proud of himself. After giving it much consideration, we agreed that Justin would ride the bus back home around 11:45 each day. Cheryl arranged her schedule to arrive at our house at 10:00 o'clock each morning. This was so she had time to get a few things accomplished before Justin got home.

I didn't know it at the time but like any good teacher, Cheryl was observing everything about our children, especially Justin. After the first week she asked Rick and me if it would be okay if *she* met Justin at the top of the driveway to help him off the bus. "I believe this would help Justin to trust me more—if he knew I would be there for him every day. Even if you're home, Mrs. Brown," Cheryl said, "I'd like to meet him. You know, until he gets used to me." We both agreed this was a good idea.

Justin loved going to school with his big brother and sister. All of Jade's friends fell in love with him right away. In fact, her fourth-grade class adopted Justin's class. They bickered over who was going to work with Justin. Jade was not allowed to work with her own brother; she had to select another child.

"Mommy, all of my friends fight over whose turn it is to play with Justin," Jade laughed, feeling proud because her little brother was so popular and cute.

Justin became quite independent and his vocabulary increased. He still didn't speak in complete sentences— just a couple of words here and there. However, his sign language improved and increased. He had many more words to choose from. He understood everything that was said to him.

One morning Jade came into Taylor and Justin's bedroom looking for her baseball socks. Justin was awake, but he was still in bed. Jade scurried around the room looking in Taylor's drawers. "Mommy, I've got a game today!" She yelled, continuing to look for the socks.

At that moment, Justin jumped out of bed as if he were in a hurry too. "I got game today!" He repeated as best he could what Jade had said loud and clear.

Jade stopped dead in her tracks and so did I. We turned to look at each other. *Did we hear the same thing?*

"Mommy!" Jade shouted. "Justin just said exactly what I said. You heard him, didn't you, Mommy?"

"Yes, I heard him say he had a game today."

Jade and I both hugged and kissed Justin. He was very proud of himself and smiled all the way to the bathroom.

Taylor was in the tub when Justin marched into the bathroom. "Why is Justin smiling so much so early in the morning?" Taylor asked.

Jade explained to him what Justin had said. "Say it again, Justin," Jade encouraged him. "Say 'I've got a game today.'"

He would not repeat it. Taylor had missed out on something really big and so had Rick. I would have given almost anything for Taylor and Rick to hear Justin repeat a complete sentence. What Jade and I heard on that very special morning was truly music to our ears.

***

"Marcia, Marcia, Marcia," Jade sang. "Mommy, that's all you've been talking about for a long time!" It was true, although I didn't realize it until she brought it up. The *Brady Bunch* movie was in the theaters and Jade had just seen it. To her it was a joke. Really the joke was on me. The real Marcia in my life was the new big shot in town from New York. She had come to make L'Agence Models number one in Atlanta. All the girls who worked through L'Agence *already* believed our agency was number one. We were there and we knew there was no question that Madeleine had the best runway girls in town. Most of us had worked in New York, Paris, or Milan at some point. We were intelligent, beautiful, and professional. Everyone talked about us; we didn't care if it was good or bad, as long as they talked.

Mark, the owner of L'Agence brought Marcia in to make sure we stayed on top and remained number one. Each girl with L'Agence had to meet with Marcia to be evaluated so to speak. This was to find their strengths. After my meeting with Marcia I had a fresh and different prospective about my career. I had gotten back into modeling just to have something fun to do and feel good about. Now, it had actually turned again into a money-making career. I loved it. It kept me young. My life was exciting again, even if it was only in Atlanta and occasional bookings in Chicago.

"You're going after the wrong market," Marcia told me, "You certainly are beautiful and glamorous, but that's not your market any longer."

"Well, what am I supposed to do?" I snapped, annoyed by her abrupt tone.

"You could make more money, Chloé, if you left fashion to the young girls. You've done that already. Move on to lifestyle and commercial."

I knew what commercial modeling was, but I didn't know anything about lifestyle modeling.

"Chloé, lifestyle is all about women. Women like you, your age, who are married with children. Women who love living a good life and like to shop and travel. This is your market." Marcia was enthusiastic and animated. Because of her excitement I gave her my undivided attention. She started flipping through a bunch of magazines pointing out what I could be doing.

"This is where the money is for you, Chloé. Forget about fashion." She picked up the phone and began dialing. As she waited for the person to answer, she bragged, "I'm calling a photographer who will test you—simply because I want him to."

She's arrogant, I thought, but I was still impressed. That's what Tiziana had done for me in Milan.

Marcia had been right. With her help and advice I tested with several wonderful photographers. She changed my entire portfolio. Once it was together, she sent it around to clients in several different cities. Because of Marcia, I began to work for clients I had never even known existed.

Marcia had two children of her own, Jake, a son Justin's age, and Morgan, a daughter a year younger. We enjoyed talking about our children—their likes and dislikes, and what they had done at different stages. We were also excited about our kids becoming friends.

Jade and Taylor always had friends over to visit, but Justin didn't. So I invited Marcia to bring her kids over to play. It was an amazing sight to behold. They bonded instantly, as though they had always known each other.

Justin, Jake, and Morgan played outside for two hours without any problems. Marcia and I sat on the deck talking as we watched the kids interacting beautifully. It was as though they were communicating in a secret language. Justin led them around. We could see he was in charge. He pointed out different things to Jake and Morgan as they walked around the play area. They swung on the swings, slid down the slide, played in the sandbox, threw balls to each other, played hide-and-seek, and rode on everything with wheels. The three of them actually walked up to the deck holding hands when it was time for lunch. Justin had his very own little friends, and they loved each other. Marcia and I both agreed the three of them were somehow spiritually connected.

***

"Why is Justin pointing to his teeth?" Brenda asked. "I know he's trying to tell me something. Did you hurt your mouth, Baby?"

"Oh no! He's not hurt," I explained, "he's telling you he's going to the dentist: He's a big boy now." Taylor and I had gone to the dentist the previous week, and now it was Jade and Justin's turn to go. We had taken Justin to watch Taylor get his teeth cleaned, so he wouldn't be so nervous when it was his turn. He shocked all of us, including the dentist, who had been our family dentist before Jade was born.

Justin was eager to sit in the chair when Taylor got up. We all laughed as the dentist held up his hand, spreading his fingers wide. "Your turn is in five days, Justin. I hope you're this excited when you come back." Justin did stay excited. He walked around for the next five days, telling everybody he was getting his teeth cleaned.

When Justin was just a month old his cardiologist had informed me to always tell his doctors and especially his dentist about his ventricular septal defect. He said they would have to give him a specific medication before they could clean his teeth or do any other dental work. The dentist phoned the cardiologist to make sure he had all the information. Then he called in a prescription Justin had to take a few hours before he could clean his teeth. Justin had his teeth officially cleaned for the first time in April, six months before his fourth birthday.

I wanted to stay in the room to watch and make sure Justin would cooperate, but Justin forced me to leave. The dental hygienist laughed. "That's the funniest thing I've seen in a long time. A lot of *adults* aren't as brave."

"Mommy's going to stand right over here, Justin," I assured him, but he waved me out, shaking his head no.

"Do you want Jade to stay with you?"

"No!" he shook his head. He was determined to get his teeth cleaned all by himself with no one standing around watching. He knew this was big and he was determined to come out a winner. I left the room but I slipped back inside when he wasn't looking.

***

Our baby boy got a kick out of going to his big brother's and sister's sports events, especially baseball.

"He should have his own uniform for both teams," everybody joked. Everyone at the ballpark knew Justin and all the other little rugrats who were too small to participate but wanted to be at every game. Justin became an honorary member of a pack of kids who roamed together. Most of them were three, four, and five years old. As soon as the game was over the pack reappeared ready for their treats. All the parents made sure to bring extra just for them.

Cheryl was definitely a Godsend. I'd never met anyone with her patience for children. She knew how to entertain them *and* keep them on the right track at the same time. She commanded respect without ever saying it. Jade and Taylor had only good things to say about her. Rick loved Cheryl's ideas regarding the children. She loved taking them places and they never got bored.

Initially, I was concerned because Justin became very disagreeable. He slapped Cheryl often; for some reason he did *not* want to be with her. She hadn't told me about the slapping. One afternoon I witnessed the abuse firsthand. The three of us were going to the market. I had just gotten into the SUV and as I put on my seatbelt Cheryl tried to put Justin into his safety seat. He didn't want her to, so he slapped her. He struck her hard bringing tears to her eyes, and also to mine. I couldn't believe it. I was in shock momentarily, but quickly stepped out of my seat. By the time I reached Cheryl's side, she assured me she could handle it. "He does that because he's frustrated, because he can't tell me in words how he feels." She never lost her composure.

I hadn't thought about that. My first response was to reprimand him to tell him how terrible he had been for hitting Cheryl. She taught me a lot that afternoon. But instead of feeling good about it, I felt sorry for myself. *Why didn't I know?*

Cheryl and Justin became friends at the baseball park. When Taylor and Jade had to be in two places at the same time, Cheryl would take one of them while Rick or I took the other. One afternoon after Justin got home from school, Cheryl told me he didn't want her to carry him down the driveway or to hold his hand any longer as they walked to the house. "He only wants to do what he sees Taylor and all the other little boys do at the ballpark."

She was right, and I was grateful she had pointed it out.

One of Justin's favorite things to do was to be pushed on the swing. But sometimes I got tired of pushing. I figured out Justin was just as happy sitting in my lap, so the two of us together swung and swung and swung. The only way I could tear him away was by saying we were going to get McDonald's French fries. This worked every time.

One late afternoon as I prepared dinner and talked to my friend Tami, I happened to look out the kitchen window. There standing in the kitchen, I witnessed a huge success; Justin was swinging all by himself—pumping his little body, swinging, swinging, swinging. I couldn't believe what I was seeing. I screamed—scaring Tami half to death.

"What's wrong?" she screamed back, grabbing me tightly. Shaken, I dropped a stack of bowls, breaking them.

"Justin is swinging all by himself!" I shouted. "Look at him! Look!" Forgetting about the broken dishes, I ran out of the house to the play area still yelling that Justin was swinging all by himself. By the time I reached Justin and Cheryl I found myself pointing at Justin out of breath with astonishment. "Look! Look at Justin, he's swinging by himself!"

Cheryl flashed a huge toothy grin and chuckled, "Yes! He sure is! He's been swinging for a few days now."

***

"An auto mechanic's body shop business! What do you know about cars besides driving them?" I couldn't believe what Rick was telling me. I thought he had actually lost his mind. As my husband tried to explain the business to me, I just thought of everything that could go wrong. "Rick, listen to me." I was very agitated because he couldn't see my perspective. "You can't just go out and buy some business dealing with cars when you don't know the first thing about repairing cars." Now we were both yelling.

I believed that in this particular situation, I was smarter than Rick. Being the analytical person that I am, I knew he would have a difficult time pulling this off. He had never had to work out any deals on his own. He had always had agents and attorneys negotiate everything for him. His entire adult life he simply sat back and waited for a phone call or a letter from the men working on his behalf. They would tell him how much money he would make and in which city or country he would be working.

In the end I had no choice but to allow Rick to call his own shots regardless of whether I believed in them or not. *He'll get the hang of it once he's done it for a while*, I said to myself. In the meantime I wanted him to hear me.

We finally agreed to listen to each other. Rick told me he wouldn't have to repair any cars. *Thank God*! I thought. "Besides" he said, "it's body work. Once you go with me to meet the owners and the people who are already working there, you'll see for yourself." I gave in and Rick called the brokers working on his behalf so they could set up an appointment for all of us to meet and discuss the business.

It was good for my family that the month of May was a very slow fashion period. I had only seven days of work in the entire month. This didn't bother me because I could stay home to help my husband find the right business to buy and run for the second chapter of his life. Retiring wasn't all it was cracked up to be, especially when you're not even forty yet. You need to continue working to maintain your lifestyle—and, in Rick's case, his manhood.

All the owners of the businesses we looked into tried to convince us theirs was the best one to buy. The body shop deal looked great at first. I gave in to the idea after seeing their set-up. A husband and wife team owned it. They had built the business from scratch seventeen years earlier. Now, they just wanted to get out and live a little. They told us they were going to take two years off and then build another one. "But don't y'all worry," they grinned. "We won't build to compete with y'all. As a matter of fact, we won't even be living in this vicinity."

Rick and I were starting to get excited. The brokers went to work drawing up the contracts. I was happy for Rick. The whole set-up seemed *do-able*: That was the word the broker used often. And another phrase was *the numbers looked great*. Rick talked about all the money he could make and how we could keep the same lifestyle that we'd always lived and enjoyed. All of the workers were in place. The owners agreed to stay on and help Rick for six months and to be consultants for another year.

But the shit hit the fan when the owners were reluctant to give Michael, our accountant, all the tax information and returned checks. He needed this information to do a proper investigation of the company. The husband flat out told him, "No!"

Six hours later the broker called saying he would agree to let Michael go through the paperwork, but only if he was allowed to stay in the room with him. "No way!" Michael complained. "I can't work like that." This was the end of that deal.

Rick and the brokers were right back where they started, looking for the right business. Rick's spirits were down. He had so much hope things would work out. However, things only got worse. I tried to keep myself busy with the children.

Justin and I had lots of fun strolling in the yard while Jade and Taylor were still in school. Of course, he wanted to swing every day, go on the slide, and ride his tricycle. We even planted more flowers near the front gate.

One day I followed Cheryl and Justin as they walked hand-in-hand. He fought with her to let it go, and she did. Another day I saw him pushing her away telling her to let him swing by himself, and she did. Sometimes Cheryl would sit on the deck and watch Justin from there. He had finally reached the point where he just wanted to do things all by himself without Cheryl or me.

***

"Justin is a good student," his teacher told me one morning as I dropped him off at school. On most mornings Rick took the children to school. It must have been a while since I had taken Justin to school. "Show your mommy how you can hang up your book bag and sweater, Justin," his teacher asked him. Justin did exactly as she had instructed him without missing a beat. "Now go over to the work table and get your work box. Then find your seat." He did just what the teacher asked him to do. I was impressed. As he walked to his seat he waved to his old friend Jasmine. She had been in his class at another school for children with delayed development.

"Hey, Justin," Jasmine said, then pointed to me. "Justin's mommy," she said. I was flattered. She and Justin sat at the same table. I liked that.

His teacher went on to tell me that Justin knew a lot of sign language. "But there's one sign I'm not sure about. When he's eating, sometimes he puts his finger to his cheek and turns it back and forward. What is he saying?" A big smile came to my face and I almost laughed out loud. I told her he had always used that sign, just as my older children had when they were toddlers.

"It's Italian," I said. "It means *the food is good*. In Justin's case, he's probably saying he wants more." She called the other teacher in the class to share this information with her.

I said good-bye and was about to leave, when Mrs. Neu stopped me. "Mrs. Brown, I think it would be a good idea if you and Mr. Brown would start letting Justin walk to class with Jade or Taylor. This would be a wonderful experience for him."

"Do you really think so?" I asked.

"I do," she said. "He's very capable of doing so much, and he's eager to learn." Then she added, "He wants to be independent you know. So this would be great for him."

"Sure, this will not be a problem. Starting tomorrow he can walk in with Jade and Taylor. I'm sure they're going to like this too."

As I walked back to the car, I kept hearing what Justin's teacher had just said.

This would be great for him. This would be great for him.

As I drove away I had a feeling I couldn't explain: It made me feel unsure of myself. *Have I been overprotective of Justin? Did Rick and I baby him too much?* I began to flash back to how Cheryl let him do more things than I did. Whenever he resisted her she didn't make a big deal out of it. She allowed him to be independent, to have more freedom.

Would Justin have learned to swing alone if I had been watching him? I remembered how afraid I was with the thought of Justin falling out of the swing and hurting himself if I weren't standing right there behind him. When he didn't want Cheryl to hold his hand any longer while walking from the school bus, she didn't make him let her. The way I would have. He told Cheryl to let him go to the play area all by himself and she did. Now his teacher was telling me it would be better if I didn't walk Justin to class.

The school was right around the corner, so it only took me five minutes to get home. But I didn't go into the house for an hour. I didn't even go into the garage. I just sat in my car with the morning sun shining down on my face. Feelings of not being the best mother I could have been to Justin overwhelmed me. I had never thought for one moment, until now, that I wasn't an exceptional mother to my children. The love I had for them was enormous and solid. I knew it would never run out. My love for Justin was even deeper because I believed he needed me more.

69

Has this belief helped to prolong his delayed development? I had so many questions and almost no answers. Sitting in the car crying wasn't getting me anywhere except depressed. Eventually I pulled the car in and parked in the garage. I felt heavy as I walked into the house. Just making it down the long corridor to my bedroom was tough. I slowly pulled the covers back and got into bed and covered my head. I was glad Rick would be out all day with his brokers looking for a business to buy. I took the phone off the hook. I curled up in bed and cried hard. Feeling sorry for myself, I felt the weight of the world on my shoulders. *Who can I talk to?* I felt lost, as if I were stuck inside a small dark box as I drifted off into a deep, deep sleep.

***

"Baby!" I called out to Rick with a quizzical look. "Are you sure we don't need to hire a professional? This is a big job for just one person." I hoped once Rick got started painting he'd realize he had made a mistake and call a professional painter. I believed it was too much for him to take on all by himself.

"No!" he insisted as he put old sheets down on the floor, with Jade, Taylor, and Justin trying to contribute. They wanted to help their daddy. This is what Jade wanted for her tenth birthday. To move out of the Jack-and-Jill suite she shared with Taylor, and on to new adventures in her own bedroom and private bathroom. She got to choose her own new furniture and would soon move into Justin's room. This adventure wouldn't have been so hectic except Jade wanted her new room painted *royal blue*. It was called some other kind of blue but I know royal blue when I see it. All of the new accessories for her room and bathroom had to be *that* color as well.

The chaos began immediately. I was shocked Rick would even consider letting the children be around royal blue paint, not to mention letting them actually help. I was speechless after that. However, before leaving them to their project I decided to find more old sheets. The least I could do was make sure the furniture and floor were covered. I went downstairs but just the thought of what was going on upstairs drove me crazy. My thoughts were getting the best of me. I didn't even want to go back upstairs so I called up on the intercom to let them know I was going to Normie's house. "Call me when you guys have finished."

When I returned later that evening, Rick and all three children were in the family room watching a movie and eating pizza. They were very relaxed. It seemed as though everything had gone well. Justin had his pizza on a paper plate. Next to the plate was a very large bowl of popcorn. Rick had popped it for everybody while they waited for the pizza to arrive. However, Justin had other ideas.

"Chloé, can you believe Justin won't give us any of the popcorn? He won't even let us put our hand in the bowl," Rick told me as I stood over Justin.

"Yeah, Mommy! He thinks it's all his. I told him he had to share." Taylor was pretty upset. All I could do was laugh. From the looks of things they had really tried their best to talk Justin into sharing the popcorn. It was unusual for him, but for some reason my baby had not shared the popcorn and definitely had no plans to share.

"What did you guys do to him while I was gone?" I asked.

"Nothing!" They spoke in unison.

With all the excitement I had almost forgotten about Jade's *royal blue* room. It was Saturday, June first, and we'd promised Jade we would have everything ready on her birthday, which was just around the corner.

"So how did the painting go?" I asked.

"Mommy, you should see my room. It looks *so* cool, Mommy."

"Let's go look at it then." I said, standing up.

"Let's go, Mommy!" Jade grabbed my wrist. "Close your eyes, Mommy, and I'll tell you when to open them. Okay, Mommy?"

I couldn't wait to see how things turned out, so I allowed her to lead me up to her room.

"What about the stairs, Jade? Can't I just close my eyes when I get to the top?" Jade giggled and said she would tell me when to pick my feet up as we walked up the stairs. As we reached the top of the stairs my heart started to pound from excitement. Everything in me hoped Rick and the children had done a good job. Rick and the boys were now following Jade with me right by her side with my eyes closed. Justin and Taylor were giggling.

"Remember, Justin," Rick cautioned. "You can't touch the walls because they're still wet." Jade told Taylor the same thing.

"Jade you don't have to remind *me*." Taylor whined.

"Are you ready, Mommy?" Jade asked.

"As ready as I'll ever be."

"Okay, you can open your eyes now!"

I had waited all day for this moment. I opened my eyes. I looked straight out in front of me, to my right, to my left, and back again. I walked into the room, and as Grandmamma Freddie would say, *for the life of me*, I could not believe my eyes. When I looked down, it was worse. The off-white carpet had spots of royal blue paint in at least ten places, maybe more. I hadn't said a word yet but when I turned to look at everyone I could see they all wanted me to say something positive.

At that very moment I remembered what my best friend Collette had told me. "You've got to let him do it, Chloé; and you've got to tell him he's doing a good job." We'd been talking about how Rick wanted to do everything around the house now that he had retired from basketball and was always home without much to do.

I wanted to cry but I didn't. Rick had totally messed up the room and allowed the children to help him. I knew we would have to buy new carpet. I also knew it would be impossible for me to live with all the royal blue paint that was sprinkled on almost every object in the room.

At least the new furniture didn't arrive early.

CHAPTER 8

Summertime

"Yeaaah! We made it! Summertime! No more school!" Jade and Taylor were ready to rock-n-roll. There were always so many fun things going on in Atlanta in the summertime. We were excited and got busy planning our summer. It was going to be wonderful.

We had plenty to do. Jade and Taylor had to get ready for summer camp. They were leaving in two weeks. This was Taylor's first sleepover camp so naturally he was a little nervous. Rick and I felt confident about him going away because we knew his big sister would watch out for him. They would be away for weeks. It was all they'd talked about since June first.

Jade had been trying to educate Taylor about what sleepover camp was really all about. "It's not like the camps on TV, Taylor." She had been getting on his nerves. Taylor just wanted her to be quiet. She was a know-it-all.

"I've seen the videotape of the camp four times already, Jade." Joan, our friend who was also the camp advisor, wanted to make sure they would feel comfortable about going away, so she'd sent them a tape of the camp. Taylor really enjoyed watching it. I already knew Jade would have a ball, and I believed Taylor would enjoy the camp as well.

All five of us drove to the camp, located in a remote part of North Carolina. We had a good time on the road trip and we happened to arrive on my birthday. Jade and Taylor wanted to check out the action. The first thing they had to do was take a swim test. There was a huge lake on the property. It was just as beautiful as it had looked in the brochures and the videotape. Taylor had never gone swimming in a lake before so naturally he was a bit leery. However, Jade was there to assure him it was no big deal. She had experienced it the year before at another camp.

Jade and Taylor's personal guide led the way down to the lake. We all followed. I could tell right away they were going to like it here. As we reached the lake Jade had no problem jumping right in for her swim test. She passed with flying colors. As she swam back to the bank and got out, she assured Taylor that the water was nice and cool.

"You can do it, Taylor. Just pretend you're swimming at home." The swim coach blew the whistle for Taylor to jump in. He was understandably hesitant.

"You don't have to do it if you don't want to swim while you're here," the coach said. At that moment it seemed Taylor realized that a summer camp without swimming would be no fun at all. He dove in. My son swam hard and fast, making all of us laugh. "Taylor, slow down. You're not in a race, man," his personal guide yelled out. Taylor passed the test.

Their guides had so many things to introduce them to, it was hard to keep up with them. Jade suggested we could walk around by ourselves. Justin wanted to stay with Taylor but we could sense that for the first time Taylor really didn't have time for his little brother. Rick and I took Justin with us to the cabins to unpack Jade and Taylor's bags.

It was difficult to leave them but they made it a bit easier when they waved goodbye and immediately ran back down to the lake. Jade jumped in a little boat with several other girls while Taylor and his personal guide went looking for the other boys who would be his cabin mates.

I felt a little sad on the way home. It was already too quiet. I knew I would miss Taylor. As soon as we took off down the long, narrow dirt road, Justin threw his blanket around his neck. He seemed to know just how to wrap it so that his favorite piece hung low enough to fall in his lap. He fell asleep on the back seat looking just like a sweet, plump cherub. Rick seemed a little sad too, but he welcomed the peace and quiet, and the extra rest he would get for three whole glorious weeks.

"And I won't have to carpool anybody anywhere."

"Aren't you forgetting somebody?" I turned to look on the back seat where Justin was still sleeping. He would be four years old in just four months.

"No way, Girl! Didn't you know, me and my baby boy gon' be hangin' out for the next three weeks?" I laughed at Rick; he rarely joked with me *like that*.

"But Justin is supposed to start going to The Suzuki Learning Center on July first."

"Not a big deal," he said. "We'll hang out after I pick him up."

Then Rick grabbed my hand. "*We're* going to hang out in the bedroom while Justin is away during the day, okay?"

"No problem," I blushed. "Let's hang out in the kitchen and the bathroom too. We may as well just *do it* everywhere."

"Hallelujah!" Rick shouted. "Now you're talkin' Baby!"

When we got back to Atlanta we stopped by Normie's house. She had told me on Saturday night she had something for me and wanted me to stop by. When she opened her front door for us a crowd was waiting to sing happy birthday to me! All of my siblings, several cousins who lived in town and a few family friends were there. It really made my day. I couldn't believe it. My *baby sister* was the sister who was least likely to cook a meal. However, on this day she had made a special dinner just for me, with a birthday cake and everything.

My cousin, Tafuma, the artist in the family, had painted an exquisite oil on canvas just for me. He called it *Cool Summers*. It depicted our childhood days growing up in Mississippi. Every summer he and all of his first cousins came from Memphis to visit Cousin Honey's, his grandmother's house. Her front yard was our hangout. In the painting, *Cool Summers,* Tafuma captured the essence of all of us when we were kids, playing a game of softball. It moved me in such a way that I cried as all the wonderful memories flooded my consciousness.

Justin loved getting all the attention, and since he was the only child there we all indulged him. His main objective was to blow out my candles. After we finished our meal, Normie placed the cake in the center of the table. It was indeed a beautiful cake. Justin must have walked around the table three or four times saying, "Cake, cake," while making the sign for *cake* as he filled his cheeks with air letting us know he wanted to blow out the candles.

"C'mon y'all," Tafuma yelled. "Let's strike a pose the way we used to when we took pictures growing up in Memphis." His camera lights started flashing as he snapped away. All of us knew exactly what he was talking about and we were more than happy to obey his command. We jumped up acting really silly, Memphis-style from the 1970s.

"Where da money?" Brenda asked. Y'all ain't doin' nothin' if y'all ain't got no money flashin' in the pictures." In the 70s our folks seem to take all of the family and club pictures flashing money. We cracked up with laughter remembering our people.

Rick didn't know what we were talking about. "I didn't grow up taking pictures like that, and neither did my people." He laughed. "Y'all lookin' like gangstas to me." Normie leaned down lower with her money in both hands while Tafuma's camera continued to flash.

"Yeah, man," Normie said to Rick. "That's the whole point. We gotta look gangsta!" That was a revelation to me because even though most tried to keep it on the down-low some of our Memphis relatives were actual small-time gangsters.

Without warning, Rick started running across the room yelling, "Justin! Don't do it, Justin!" Justin was standing up in one of the dining room chairs with both hands, reaching out for *my* cake. Rick's shout startled Justin, making him lose his balance. He and the chair came tumbling down. Thanks to Rick and his quick response he got to the chair and Justin before they hit the floor. We thought Justin would be shaken. Instead he didn't miss a beat, repeating, "Cake, cake," making the sign for *cake* again while filling his cheeks with air. He was absolutely determined. We blew the candles out together.

***

One week after Jade and Taylor had been at camp Rick's mother and sisters called from California, each on a different extension. They were on a mission, and they had no intention of giving up until their mission had been accomplished.

"You guys need to let those kids come out here to visit with us. They don't even know us," one of them said, through what sounded like a snotty nose and tears.

"That's not exactly true," I told them. I reminded them they had seen the children every year in May for the Brown family reunion in Mississippi. At this point they all began speaking at the same time.

Rick's mother's sweet voice prevailed. "Now, Chloé and Rick, y'all know that ain't right. Y'all need to let them kids come on out here to spend some time with us." Her cry seemed soggy and remorseful. *She seemed to have been crying a lot the last few times we had spoken. Was she trying to get her way?*

Rick told me years ago he only went to Mississippi State University because his mother cried alligator tears. She told him if he didn't play college basketball in Mississippi she would never get to see him play. He told her she could see him play on television. According to Rick, that didn't work. She only cried harder. So he gave in to the tears.

She got her way this time, too. Rick and I agreed to send Jade and Taylor to the San Francisco Bay Area after they returned home from camp.

"What about Justin?" Rick's youngest sister, Vertis, asked, and they all seemed to hold their breath waiting for the answer.

My mother-in-law spoke up. "I sho' would like to see my grandbaby. They say he look like you, Chloé."

"Momma, you should see him," Vertis broke in. "To me he looks like Daddy."

I love and adore my mother-in-law and my sisters-in-law. But when they all started to talk about Justin like that I just couldn't take it anymore.

"Well, you guys can just get the thought of Justin coming anywhere without Rick or me out of your heads. That's not going to happen." I became very agitated and said again with authority, "No, Justin *will not* be coming to visit you this summer!" I told them I had to go. Rick stayed on the phone with them for a while longer to work out the details for Jade and Taylor.

I tried to avoid Rick for the rest of the afternoon. I didn't want him to feel as though he was in the middle of anything. Later that night Rick came to me, put his arms around my waist, and hugged me.

"I understand," he said.

We were at ease as the long summer days lingered. We spoke with Jade and Taylor only on Sundays. These were the camp rules. Taylor missed his turn in line so we didn't get to speak with him the first Sunday, but Jade gave us a full report. "Everything's going great, Mommy." They had been rehearsing for a play, and according to Jade, she and Taylor both had good parts.

The second week we had the good fortune of speaking with both of them. This is when Rick announced they were going to get to go to California. They didn't seem to care and changed the subject. They both wanted to know what Justin had been doing.

"Taylor. Do you remember the day camp you went to last summer?" Rick asked.

"Yes, I had fun there, Daddy and I got to come home every day." It sounded like he was getting homesick.

"Well, Justin is going to this same day camp where you went last year, Taylor. He loves it, and he's having a good time."

"Daddy," Jade asked, "Does Justin miss us?"

"Yes, Jade! So much, he's been going into your room a lot." Jade didn't like that at all.

"Daddy! Don't let Justin go into my room! Please Daddy! He's going to mess it up."

"There's nothing to mess up, Jade. Anyway he just *looks* around the room. I think he's seeing how different it looks now that you're living there," Rick reminded her. "Remember, Jade, it used to be Justin's room."

Taking Justin to the Suzuki Learning Center was the best thing we did for him that summer. He grew so much, and the teachers there were wonderful. The director thought it would be good for Justin to be with boys and girls his own age. Rick and I loved it; and more importantly, Justin loved it even more.

I loved it when I walked into his classroom to pick him up at the end of the day. Usually he would be interacting with the other kids. His teacher told us they all got along very well. "Justin understands everything and I treat him the same as I do all the other children." I loved his teacher for that. It seemed to be just what he needed and wanted.

81

Each day she had something different and exciting to share with us. On one particular day she surprised me. "Mrs. Brown, Justin is sitting over there. He's in a time-out!"

I couldn't believe it. "Wait. What? Justin is in a time-out? Why?"

"He and another little boy were fighting over a Big Wheel bike outside. The other little boy was in a time-out, too. His dad has already picked him up."

Justin's expression told me he was guilty. When I approached him he lowered his head. "Justin, I'm disappointed. You know Mommy doesn't like fighting."

Justin had a sad but sweet look on his face. He stood up and brought his hand up to my face. *I'm sorry*, he said. Justin's way of apologizing was by rubbing my face gently in a circular motion.

"Get your bag, please." I commanded him. He walked into the room where all the bags hung on hooks, looked around the room for a minute and found his hook. *Justin sure is cute in a time-out.*

After he was settled into his car seat comfortably he fumbled through his book bag and took out his blankie. Exhausted, Justin threw the blanket around his neck and sat back to relax for the short ride home. I looked at him all the way home in the rearview mirror. I thought of all the progress he had made in such a short time and of how cute he looked with his blanket wrapped around his neck like a shawl. *I'm going to have to cut that blanket into smaller pieces. He's getting too big to drag that big thing around everywhere he goes.*

***

When we picked Jade and Taylor up from camp they smelled awful, and I did not hesitate to let them know. "Mommy, this is how everybody smells," Jade informed us.

"Yeah, Mommy," Taylor chimed in and actually bragged. "Everybody smells just like me and Jade."

Justin wanted to know if he smelled as badly as Jade and Taylor. "Me too?" he asked.

"No way! Mommy's baby doesn't smell like the swamps. You smell nice and clean, Justin. Just like Mommy and Daddy."

After being home for only a few days, Jade and Taylor packed up again and flew out to San Francisco. Taylor didn't really want to go, but Jade talked him into going with her. That is, after Rick and I talked *her* into going. They had both gone before with Rick, but never alone. Jade had flown alone before, but this flight would be quite an adventure for her since she would be in charge of herself and her little brother.

"Mommy, tell Taylor he has to listen to me."

"Taylor you have to listen to Jade. Okay?"

Taylor said, "okay," but he really wasn't listening to anyone at this point. His mind was on all the new games I had packed for him.

After hearing they had arrived safely in San Francisco, Rick and I were relieved and happy we'd agreed to allow the children to travel to California to visit the Brown side of the family. Taylor called us every day—and from every house he visited. He said he was lonely and there were no boy cousins to play with. After Taylor visited all his aunts, his grandmother, and even got into a couple of fights with his girl cousins (there are seven of them), he was ready to come home.

On the other hand, Jade was having the time of her life. Erica, a cousin a couple of years older than she was, actually taught her to sing. Jade seemed truly happy everywhere. Our daughter is outgoing and likable; and at that point she'd never had a problem getting along with anyone.

Taylor started calling his grandmother "Daddy's mother." Not happy, he told us he would rather stay with Aunt Linda. So Rick's sister Linda drove to Sacramento to bring Taylor back to the Bay Area with her, where he stayed until his return flight to Atlanta.

We really missed them. They ended up being gone at least half the summer.

***

We had been telling Justin for two long days that his big brother and sister were finally coming home. We arrived at the airport in Atlanta early and went right to the gate where Jade and Taylor would arrive. We wanted to be there for them as they walked off the plane.

After about thirty minutes the first person off the plane finally appeared. Rick roared, "Here they come, Justin!" He held Justin up as he pointed toward Jade and Taylor walking out. They still hadn't seen us yet. Justin was ecstatic and struggled to get away from his daddy's grip. He wanted to run to his sister and brother. Rick intended to let him tear away from his grip at the right moment. The two of us smiled broadly as we watched Justin run through the crowd. When he reached Jade he grabbed her legs and wouldn't let go until he saw Taylor. It was a picture so beautiful it should have been in a movie. Several other people waiting at the gate got warm fuzzy feelings just watching our children—and then our whole family—come together.

I realized just how much Justin had truly missed them. The five of us must have done our group hug and dance for at least two or three minutes. I had never seen Justin so excited. He wanted to say so much but his muscles and delayed development wouldn't allow him. Still, he did the best he could.

After all the hugging and kissing, Taylor looked at us slightly irritated and said, "We've been gone from home *too long*!"

"For real, Mommy!" Jade said, apparently feeling the same way. "We don't want to stay away that long *no more*. Okay, Mommy?"

"I know how you guys feel," I assured them. Rick and I had already decided that from now on one trip per summer for the kids would be enough. We had all missed each other way too much. As we walked away from the arrival gate at the airport and back to the train we watched as all three of our children strolled ahead of us hand-in-hand, with Justin in the middle.

As we rode on the train and waited for it to arrive at baggage claim Taylor and Jade couldn't get enough kisses from Justin. Each time they asked him for a kiss he'd tilt his little face upward so they could get as many kisses as they wanted. I adored the fact that Justin never turned us down when we wanted to plant a kiss on his cheek. Even when he had considered himself preoccupied or in a hurry, he would pucker up his lips, smooch us quickly, then push us away and go on about his business.

***

During the next two and half weeks, we had the best time of our lives as a family. The 1996 Olympic Games were practically in our backyard. We had looked forward to being a part of it since Jade and Taylor were babies. It was finally here!

My friend Collette came to stay with us for ten days. We set out to take advantage of our once-in-a-lifetime opportunity. We all agreed we were going to behave like tourists in Atlanta by taking the train and looking all around as we walked around downtown and took in all the special events around town. It was incredibly fun.

Taking the train reminded me of being in Paris and Milan. We had never heard so many different languages and accents all in one place before. Rick, Collette, the kids, and I played a game. We tried to figure out where all the people were from after hearing them speak. Everywhere we went everyone was so nice and friendly. Almost all the people we spoke to had come from another country, and they all made comments on the American flag scarves Jade and Taylor were wearing on their heads. Collette had brought them with her from New York and the kids thought they were cool. Especially after so many people asked about them and told them how *American* they looked.

We wore ourselves out. We went to women's volleyball and baseball, women's and men's basketball, wrestling, weight-lifting, diving and several different events for track and field. Of course, there were lots of free events and parties, and we participated in as many as we could fit into our days and nights. I thought the kids would pass out but they didn't. They continued to hang with us every step of the way.

Whew! What a summer! And we still had more to see and do. Taylor's birthday was coming up the first week of August, which was just after the Olympics. Collette decided to stay for his birthday celebration and take a flight back to New York later that night. We wanted to make Taylor's seventh birthday celebration truly special. We invited his cousin Lloyd, his neighborhood friends, and all of his baseball buddies. Earlier in the spring Taylor's baseball team had gone undefeated and won the championship in their division.

Justin knew all of Taylor's buddies. He actually believed he was on their level, and that they were his buddies, too. The boys were very sweet and allowed Justin to have his way whenever he wanted to take the bat and not share. They were smart kids and knew just what to do. They would pitch to Justin until he got tired. Believe me, they knew just how to wear him out. Sure enough, eventually Justin would throw the bat down and run off to do something else. The moment the bat hit the dirt the boys would all cheer and say, "Let's play ball, men!"

Rick and I videotaped the party and took lots of photographs. Justin was tall for his age and was happy to point out to some of the boys that he was as big as they were.

When it was time for Taylor to open his presents all his friends gathered around him as they piled his gifts on the table. As Taylor opened each present the boys yelled out what they thought was underneath the wrapping paper.

"Don't try to guess what it is, boys," I suggested. "Let Taylor find out. It's his gift." But they didn't listen. These boys were real boys and their energy seemed to be bursting out of the house.

Finally, Taylor opened every present. I brought out the cake. They all started huffing and puffing, including Justin. I tried to explain to Justin, "This is Taylor's birthday and this is *his* birthday cake. Taylor gets to blow the candles out, not you." I already knew this could be problematic because of what happened with my own birthday cake. But I never imagined I would need to say this same thing to a group of six- and seven-year-olds. In fact, all of the boys who were close enough to blow out the candles filled their cheeks with air and blew. Taylor was annoyed, but soon realized he was having too much fun for his anger to last for more than a minute.

Justin kept repeating, "My birthday, my birthday," making the sign for *cake* and pretending to blow out candles. Rick and I couldn't wait for Justin's own birthday party. It would be Rick's first year at home with Justin on his birthday. Justin was definitely ready for a big celebration of his own and he certainly deserved one.

"Justin!" Rick called to him holding up two fingers, "Your birthday is in two months." Justin held up two fingers as well. Just like the sign for *peace*.

"Yes, Justin!" I said, "In two months Mommy, Daddy, Jade, and Taylor, and all of your friends will come to *your* birthday party, okay?"

"Okay!" Justin shouted with a gigantic grin on his face. He threw his head back and spun himself around with excitement.

***

Atlanta's fall fashion season kicked off in late August, the last Monday of the month. Socialites and fashion groupies could hardly wait for the big reveal from Jeffrey Fashion Cares' show and fundraising event.

"Hey girl!" Madeleine, my agent was her perky self. "I've got you booked!" Giggling, I grabbed my agenda as Madeleine began reading off her list. I was booked solid for the next three weeks with fashion shows and lifestyle photography shoots. I loved the energy this time of year, and could hardly wait to see all the girls and guys in fashion again. Of course, this was nothing like kicking off the fall fashion season in Milan, but nevertheless, I loved it!

Earlier in the summer I began a new healthy lifestyle routine. On Mondays, Wednesdays and Fridays I dutifully pulled myself out of bed at 5:00 in the morning to make myself eat grits and egg whites. Twenty-five minutes later I was off to meet Steve, my new personal fitness trainer. I saw an article about him and his services in *Vogue* and knew I wanted him as my trainer. Steve's only prerequisite for me was, "Don't bother to show up if you don't eat first." He told me to eat the grits and egg whites. I did it. I wanted to accomplish my goals and please Steve, but I didn't like eating so early in the morning. My warm-ups began promptly at 6:00 AM and I was on time.

I caught Rick giving me a few side eyes those first few mornings. First off, he was in shock I was actually getting up so early to do anything that wasn't for the children or modeling. I was born a night person. I never wanted to get up early for anything, so this was a surprise even for me. But this was my choice and I was in charge. I was creating my own life. So I did it and loved it. I was exhilarated and committed to what I believed in.

School was going to start again on September third. I realized I needed to go shopping for everyone. "Okay, you guys. You're wearing me out." I told Rick and the kids as I tried to think of something special to do for his thirty-eighth birthday; which was coming up in a few days, the end of August. Rick told me not to stress myself out about it, because he'd already been celebrating all summer. *Cool,* I thought, relieved.

We had a small and quiet dinner with just the kids and the two of us. The next day, we took the kids shopping for new school clothes. Justin was extremely excited. This would be his first time picking out clothes he liked. He tried them on just like Taylor and Jade did. Rick and I enjoyed it, but we were completely worn out. We were finally ready for summer to be over so the children could get back in school again, and we could wind down and get back to business.

Jade and Taylor loved school. They were both excited to see all of their friends. We still hadn't made a clear decision about Justin yet. We had two excellent options. We were impressed with Mrs. Neu, Justin's teacher from the previous year, but had not met his new teacher for the upcoming year. The best thing about his returning is that Jade and Taylor would be there with him. Rick and I had discussed it over the last three days. We wanted to make the right decision for our baby boy. I believed with all my heart that if Justin had the right assistance, teachers, speech therapist, and physical therapist, he would catch up and be ready to blend in with his class by first grade.

"We don't need to stress about this, Chloé," Rick assured me. "We'll make a final decision the night before school starts." I agreed. I could finally relax.

Rick and I were determined to make Saturday a relaxing day. He and the children swam all day. They took advantage of the last long summer weekend before school started again. I made fruit snacks and sandwiches for them and made sure they had lots of cold beverages to drink. Jade took her boom box to the pool and played the music extremely loud. It was definitely a party.

Justin was in his favorite place and with his favorite people. I looked down at them from the kitchen window. Justin never wore swim trunks and this day was no different. I saw Jade struggling with him, trying to put on his new trunks. She insisted. "You're too big to swim without your trunks. You're a big boy now!" Justin knew everyone else wore them but for some reason he always resisted. I thought he had associated being in the pool with being in the tub but by now he certainly knew the difference.

I have to talk to Justin about that. Jade is right. He's a big boy and he needs to cover his private parts. He's not in Europe. I giggled and smiled to myself.

***

I had spent nearly twenty-four hours reflecting on Justin's life once Rick and I returned to the hospital. He was our baby boy. Our special, sweet baby boy.

Whenever Rick came home, even if he had only been away for an hour, not to mention days or weeks, Justin would take off running toward his daddy. And every single time, Rick said the same thing: "There's my baby boy!"

Justin wasn't special because he was born with a heart defect and defeated it. He wasn't special because he had a muscle disorder and he was living with it. He wasn't special because of the unfortunate setbacks that took place in his life. In spite of all of those things he was special from the very beginning.

The Brown Family on a bike ride with
Justin at age two and a half.

Justin, one month before his untimely death
and three months before his 4ᵗʰ birthday

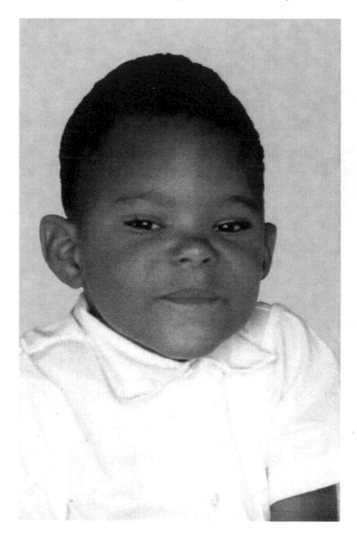

The Brown children, Jade, Taylor and Joshua

Chloe and Rick enjoying
an Atlanta Hawks basketball game

CHAPTER 9

Praying for a Miracle

Justin was courageous and sweet, with just the right amount of mischief for a little boy. He never complained, and more often than not he had a grin or a cute smirk on his face.

All of the decisions Rick and I had made on behalf of our baby boy had worked out for him and for our family until now. We had been very hopeful and encouraged that he would continue to grow and learn how to work around his challenges and delayed development. We believed he would have an opportunity to create a wonderful life for himself, just as Jade and Taylor would.

Now, we had to make the hardest decision of our lives. Rick and I were standing near Justin's bed, praying for a miracle. All of Justin's doctors, and Lin, his nurse at the hospital, were there going about their work. I looked at each of them. *How can they take this? Babies and children were dying in Intensive Care Unit day after day. What does this do to them?*

I don't remember which doctor spoke first, but they were all in agreement. They told us that life support wasn't going to make Justin better, and that he wasn't going to get better on his own. "Justin will continue to breathe with the life support, but we don't know for how long," Doctor Goldstein explained. He reminded us, "Justin's life could continue but only in a vegetative state."

They wanted us to think about disconnecting the life support. I looked into Justin's pediatrician's eyes for something, anything, some kind of hope. I saw compassion but no encouragement to hold out for a miracle.

As I stood over my baby's bed I couldn't see him because my own hot, salty tears blinded me. *This can't be it. This can't be the end.* From the very beginning my son had been a fighter. Even in my womb. I remember hemorrhaging without warning in Spain, and the doctors saying they would have to do a D and C if the bleeding didn't stop. It did stop. Justin survived.

And now this, Lord! You allowed Justin to be born and now you're just letting him die? How am I ever going to go on with my life? What about Rick and Jade and Taylor? This is something I will never get through. Please God! Not my baby!

I thought about Jade and Taylor at school. "How will Jade and Taylor go on, Rick? What are we going to tell them?"

"We're going to get through this, Chloé." Rick tried to reassure me as he wept, pulling me close into his chest.

I believed Justin would be with God, Jesus, all the angels, and all the saints. But that was no comfort to me. He died. Five days later on Friday, September thirteenth. It was five weeks before his fourth birthday. He wouldn't get to have his birthday party or the opportunity to blow out his very own candles as I had promised.

Will he have a birthday cake in heaven?

CHAPTER 10

Momma

Rick and I usually entered our home through the garage or the side door, but we walked through the front door after Justin's memorial services. I knew things would never ever be the same again. I didn't know how long it would take before my complete nervous breakdown would occur. But I knew from the bottom of my heart that it was coming.

Even though I had been comforted for over two weeks by the constant love and support of so many family members and friends, I was still very sad and suffering. I was indeed a broken woman. My paradigm had crashed into more than a million little pieces with jagged edges that could never be put together again. Aunt Anita had been with me since the accident, but now she and Uncle Arvern had to return to their lives in Mississippi. Rick's mother and father were leaving too, and so was his sister Linda. My sisters and brothers stayed awhile, and many friends did, too.

I escaped to my bedroom, too weak and broken even to thank my family and friends for being there for me. I crawled into my bed with my creamy white pantsuit still on that I had worn to the services. I cried deep, long, and hard, like a wailing animal. My pillow was a soggy mess. I remembered Lin's embrace in the hospital. I wanted arms like hers around me, to hold me and tell me she would be there as long as I needed it. But very quickly, reality set in. There would be no one to fill those shoes.

"Momma!" I sobbed profusely. "I want you!" I believed at this moment that Momma, only *my* momma, could help me cope and get through this nightmare. I wanted her to hug and caress me the way she did when I was a little girl. I wanted her to rub my hair gently as she held me close to her bosom. I wanted her to tell me we were going to get through this together, that she wouldn't leave me, and that she would stay with me as long as I wanted her to stay. But that would never happen. It was impossible.

***

It had been a long, hot Mississippi summer in 1971. By August all of us kids were getting restless and ready to do something else. We were even up for going back to school if necessary. There was nothing else to look forward to. On August first, I had a brainstorm to create some excitement. Momma's birthday was in two days. *I'm gonna throw Momma a surprise birthday party*! I didn't have a clear picture of how I would pull it off since we didn't have anything in the house to create a party. I needed to get to the store, but I didn't drive and didn't have anyone to drive me. On top of that, I didn't have any money to buy anything for the party once I got there. My major concern was the cake. I knew if I could only come up with one thing, it had to be the cake.

What would a party be without a cake? I didn't know how to make cakes from scratch like so many of the other girls in the neighborhood, so I desperately needed to get to the store. But it was too far to walk. I slept on my idea for two nights and still didn't have a plan. I couldn't tell anyone else either, because no one felt the way I did. Plus, they didn't know how to keep a secret.

Finally, it was the day. August third. Momma's birthday! I woke up early but not early enough to say happy birthday to her. She had already left for work by the time I got up. I was on a mission this day. No one was going to get in my way, either. I questioned all the people I came in contact with about their plans for the day. By now I had to tell somebody about the party if I was going to pull it off, so I started inviting them to come over. Everyone was happy to receive an invitation. May I remind you that all of these people were kids—children ranging from age seven to seventeen.

I don't remember how I got to the store this magical day or where I got the money from to purchase my meal, but I did it. I bought a mix for a strawberry cake, some potatoes, string beans, and a chicken to fry. We already had eggs and corn meal for a pan of corn bread. What a great party I was planning.

As I stood in the kitchen peeling the potatoes, my big brother Raymond walked in the back door with his friends from the neighborhood. They were good boys and had always treated me especially nice, although a little aggravation was normal just to remind me that I was still a little snotty-nosed girl to them. Raymond's friends stayed the entire time I was in the kitchen cooking. I don't think they believed I could pull it off.

My brother's friend Newt was my favorite, and Momma thought he was kind of special too. He was constantly in and out of the kitchen trying to tell me what to do. He convinced me to let him show me how to spread the frosting on the cake. He *said* he knew how to make it look like the cakes on television. What a mistake! He was heavy-handed, spreading the frosting so hard he tore a hole in the cake. I was crushed! I took the knife out of his hand, threw him out of the house, and patched up Momma's cake as best I could.

Everybody showed up on time for the party. Of course they would; there weren't many parties going on in our neck of the woods. In fact, Momma never had a birthday party for me or for any of my brothers and sisters. Well, I'll be fair and say that I don't remember her throwing a party for any of us. I instructed all of the little kids eight and under to go up the hill to Cousin Ruthie's house, which sat directly above our house on the hill, which looked over several houses and the road. It was perfect for nosey neighbors. I needed somebody to watch out for Momma's car. They were more than happy to oblige me this afternoon. I knew that visions of my pink cake gave them the necessary incentive to go along with my demands.

When the children saw Momma's light blue 1969 Impala coming down the road they created a stampede getting back to our house. The looks on their faces were wild and exhilarating. Just as the last kids were running down the hill, Momma got a glimpse of them as she was pulling into our driveway. She saw the looks of excitement on their faces, but to her it must have looked like the fear of something truly horrible. She was afraid something awful had happened. She jumped out of the car and rushed into the house so quickly, she knocked the garbage can over at the back door. This was perfect. "Now!" I whispered to the children. "It's time. Yell as loud as you can!"

"*SURPRISE* and *HAPPY BIRTHDAY!*"

Initially Momma was in shock. Then she quickly realized what was happening and was relieved, and very surprised. I watched her expressions as she interacted with all of us. I knew my mother was happy and proud of me.

The party was wonderful. Everybody had plenty to eat, talked loudly, played Momma's 45 records, and danced our hearts away. I felt really special. My heart was full of love and admiration for her. I just looked at her proudly and smiled. With the loud music going and all the other kids distracted and trying to get their piece of the strawberry cake I'd promised them, I mouthed to her, *I love you Momma.*

There wasn't one other adult at Momma's surprise party. I don't know why I didn't think to invite some of *her* friends, but I know she had a wonderful time, laughing the whole time we danced. All the food was gone except for a small piece of cake. I insisted she take it to work so she could share and show her friend, Miss Irma, that *her* daughter had baked a pink cake just for her. I knew Miss Irma would be impressed and appreciate what I had done for her friend.

Momma made my big brothers Raymond and Ben clean the kitchen and dining room. She told the other kids it was time for them to go home now. "It's getting late and yawl's mommas don't know anything about my birthday party." She closed the door after saying good-bye to the last kid. Exhausted from a long day at work and her party, she plopped down on our green leather sofa, let out a big sigh, and began to cry softly.

At first I wasn't sure why she was crying. I didn't want her to be sad. Just as I was about to speak and ask her what was wrong, she grabbed my hand and patted the sofa for me to sit next to her. She gave me a real tight bear hug and kissed me. It felt so good and real to be loved. She told me how much the party meant to her and how proud she was of me. "I had no idea you were plannin' a party for me. How did you keep it a secret?"

My mother and I stayed up late after everyone else had gone to bed. We didn't talk much, but we enjoyed each other's company. She seemed truly happy. The next thing I knew it was morning and I was in my bed. Momma had already left for work and things were back to normal again.

Around August fifteenth all of the neighborhood kids ended up at Pearl Nealey's house. Pearl was a very soft-spoken friendly lady with seven or eight children of her own, all about the same ages as my brothers and sisters. Her oldest son Little Jr. and my brother Raymond were very close.

On this particular day there must have been about twenty to twenty-five neighborhood kids at her house. We were having a ball. The boys had started a basketball game and all of the girls began cheering for their special team. I chose the same team as my favorite cousin Linda. We had everything going for us except cheerleading uniforms. The guys were sweating and playing ball as if their lives depended on it, and the girls were jumping up and down doing splits and the whole nine yards. Miss Pearl even sent someone to bring sodas down for everybody. It couldn't have been a more perfect sunny summer day for a bunch of country kids who had a few more days of fun before school started again. I was cheering for Raymond's team. He made a great pass to Little Jr., and he scored. We jumped up and down, did splits, special kicks and screamed as though we were at a high school tournament. We were having the time of our country lives, and taking this game very seriously. The next time our team got the ball we knew something special was about to happen.

All the boys were glistening with sweat as it rolled down their faces and off their backs. I noticed Miss Pearl's husband walking toward us as we cheered. Then he moved on past us girls to the boys on the dirt basketball court. He motioned for his son, Little Jr., to come over to him. The boys on the dirt court didn't miss a beat. They continued to play. The ball was passed in and all eyes were on the receiver. He then passed the ball very quickly to Raymond, who dribbled up the court trying to figure out what to do next. He decided he was going to take the shot.

Just as he was about to go for the basket, Little Jr. came over to him and said something into his ear. Raymond continued to dribble as he listened and Little Jr. whispered. I thought they were trying to figure out another play to defeat the opposing team; but from that point on everything came to me in slow motion. My brother started falling to the ground with the ball still in his hands. There he was, bent over in the dirt with his head almost touching the ground. I knew something was wrong. Everybody gathered around Raymond, looking down at him as though he were about to take his last breath. I started screaming, "What's wrong?"

No one said a word to me. All I got were horrified looks.

I screamed out again, "*WHAT'S WRONG? WHAT HAPPENED? WILL SOMEBODY TELL ME WHAT'S WRONG?*" Everybody stood still in silence.

Just as I was about to yell the same words again, my cousin Linda blurted out, "*Janice is dead*! *She was in a car crash on the way home from work!*"

Everyone was silent. I wanted her to take those words back and stop playing this stupid joke on me. I wanted her to tell me what was really going on. Then she said it again, but not as loudly. "*Janice is dead.*"

So many people were there all of a sudden. It seemed like there were hundreds of people around all us kids now. Children and grown folks who associated themselves with my family. Momma's friends and Grandma's friends were there as well.

I finally got the courage to look at my big brother. I believed his reaction to all of this would let me know if the madness were really true. Just as this thought came to my mind Raymond looked at me as though his life was over. My heart fell to the very same dirt where just a moment earlier we had all jumped, danced, and played.

My brother got up from the ground and grabbed my arm. We walked with the crowd of people who were on their way to Grandma's house. My heart was shattered. I was so afraid.

By the time the crowd reached Grandma's house, nobody was talking. I remembered seeing Little Jr. whisper words to Raymond but I couldn't make out what he was saying. By now I had made up in my mind that this gray cloud hanging over me was totally unreal. Made up. A mistake. *My Momma*? *Dead*? *No way*!

Just as I finished these thoughts someone ran over to the car we were in and opened the door. It felt like we all stepped out of the car simultaneously. There were so many people standing in Grandma's yard it frightened me.

Then I saw her. Grandma. Crying, yelling, screaming, throwing her arms up into the air, pacing in the front yard. Her friends were right there with her, beside her, all around her. Miss Ophelia, Grandma's friend, was there. She seemed to be marching in the yard and shouting, "Soldier! Soldier! Soldier!" I didn't know it at the time but found out later that she had been calling on God's soldiers to help my Grandma.

When all of this registered in my mind I knew it was really *for real*. My Momma was *dead*! Gone, *really dead*! I had never in my life felt that kind of pain before, and it came upon me very quickly. It was the kind of pain that can't be fixed with medication, rest, food, or anything else. It was raw, drawn out, agonizing pain, pulling at the pieces of my already shattered heart.

I thought it wasn't fair for me to be suffering this way. But in fact, at that same moment there were seven other children feeling this same incurable pain. They had names like Raymond, Ben, Curtis, Ed, Brenda, Cherrie, and Momma's baby, Normie. We were lost, in shock, and very frightened. We knew and everybody else knew that our daddy wasn't going to step forward, stop being an alcoholic, get a job, and take care of his eight children. That was out of the question. Daddy had been a nonfunctioning human being for at least the last three years. His alcoholism had destroyed his marriage with our mother and was now killing him.

There was a lot of whispering going on so I couldn't clearly hear what was being discussed, but Grandma kept repeating, "I don't want my daughter's children goin' to no poor house!" I had never seen her this way before and sensed she was about to lose control; but Miss Ophelia acted quickly. She grabbed Grandma by both arms and pulled her down onto the steps of the front porch and sat there with her. They wept bitterly yet lovingly together, holding onto each other as if their very lives depended upon it. They seemed afraid to let go.

Grandma's house had always smelled sweet. Even though she wasn't a great cook, she loved baking. There were molasses cakes, sweet potato pies, blackberry pies, peach cobbler, and sugar cookies. Baked sweet potatoes were a staple of hers; they were always freshly baked and placed on top of the stove for the taking. But this day—the very same day that had earlier been filled with sunshine and the innocence of children laughing on a dirt basketball court—had turned into a heavy, eerie, gray night. The rumbling of my stomach caused me to search the kitchen for food. I thought I would grab a sweet potato or two. But oddly there was no bowl on the stove and no sweet potatoes to be found. *This tragedy had stolen the sweet aroma from Grandma's home.*

My hunger pangs were minuscule compared to what was happening all around me. I gave up the idea of eating. *I don't care if I don't ever eat again. I don't want my momma to be dead.* I just wanted to find a place to lie down and cry myself to sleep forever.

Grandma's house had always been a refuge for me. It had been the perfect home. Now it seemed very small. Trying to find a place for eight extra people to sleep made Grandma cry again. Really, my poor grandmother never stopped crying that day. She was completely inconsolable.

I couldn't take it any longer. Seeing my Grandmother so out of control made me feel like I'd lost everything. I slipped into her bedroom and stretched out across the bed. *They'll find me later.* Ben must have been thinking the same thing. A few minutes later he came in and stretched out on the bed right beside me. He put his right arm around my shoulders and gave me a little hug. Ben wasn't the hugging type, but that little gesture saved me from being eaten up by the day's misfortunes. For the first time since I'd heard the news I didn't feel so alone. My brother was with me.

CHAPTER 11
Anywhere But Here

*I survived Momma's death. How did I do that? What did I do?
I've got to remember what I did. I was miserable for years. But
I got through it. I felt so unloved, unwanted, and poor. But I
did get through it. It was because the years passed. It was time
that eased the pain. But Justin is—I mean, he was—my baby.
I'm never going to get over this! I'm scared. I can't hang on for
the time to pass. I can't stay in this house. I don't want to be by
myself. I wish I had somebody, somebody like Momma. But I
didn't have Momma when Momma died. I'm going crazy. I've
got to get out of this house. Go somewhere! Anywhere but here!*

I was determined to get out of the house and go back
to work immediately. In fact, I showed up at Neiman
Marcus to do a fashion show at 9:00 the very next morning
after Justin's funeral services. Madeleine had given me the
booking weeks in advance. I was sure they had replaced me,
expecting me not to show up for work so soon. I didn't even
bother to phone the agency to tell them I was going in for
the show. I didn't want to take the chance of having them
tell me I'd been replaced. I knew if I stayed in the house just
one day after the funeral it would be enough to destroy me.

Everyone in the store's fashion department and all the models were shocked to see me walking in that morning. They hugged me and told me how sorry they were.

"Thank you." I accepted their condolences and kept on moving. I didn't want to talk a lot. Of course, no one really knew what to say to me anyway so I made it easier for them by not engaging them. I couldn't anyway. This was the most difficult fashion show of my entire career. It seemed to drag on for hours, but actually the show itself was less than thirty minutes. As I walked down the runway I believed everyone knew about my situation. I felt as though I was going to have a panic attack. But still, I rationalized that such a possibility would have been better than having an attack at home, alone, with no one to help me.

After suffering through that show I knew I had to get out of Neiman Marcus as quickly as I could. I felt claustrophobic. I was having trouble breathing. Just as I threw my model's bag over my shoulder to leave the store, Amy, the fashion director, asked if I would like to stay for some informal modeling. I was hesitant. I needed some air.

Many models only did this type of work to pay the rent. Others did it for the thirty-percent discount, and others did it simply because it was modeling. None of the girls I knew really enjoyed it, and right now this was the last thing I wanted to do. Unlike fashion shows, which are fast, punchy, and energetic, informal modeling pays considerably less, can drag on from one to three hours, and usually involves some personal contact with customers who are shopping, which entails a short conversation about the garment or the designer.

"You're my favorite, Chloé," Amy said with a cute smile on her face. I knew I couldn't withstand any type of fake interaction. Just before I could respond, Tami chimed in. She knew me well. Seeing that I was about to lose control she rushed over to me and grabbed my arm. "I promised Chloé I would take her to lunch," she lied. I did end up going to lunch with her, and with a few other models who had spent long hours with me at the hospital. At the restaurant, they ate. I smoked.

I stayed out of the house until it was time for Rick and me to pick up Jade and Taylor from school. Angela and Collette were still in town so they were at our home as well. That night Angela, Collette, and Vicki begged me to go out to dinner with them and devised a scheme to get me out of the house to breathe, but most importantly, they wanted me to eat. I had lost ten pounds, which is a lot for me. I had always been naturally thin, so now I looked emaciated.

Going out to a restaurant was the last thing I wanted to do. I declined. Rick insisted, "Chloé, please go. Baby, you've got to eat, even if it's just a little bit."

I finally gave in. We went to a very nice restaurant in Buckhead. I'd heard the food was amazing. I couldn't eat very much at all. I still had no appetite. I loved these women and I knew they loved me. It was killing them to see me this way. Naturally they tried everything that night to cheer me up. However, I felt incredibly guilty just for being out. When one of them said something funny, I let out a little giggle. When I thought of what I had done the guilt was enormous. I felt I was betraying Justin. "What if someone sees me laughing?" I asked. They seemed shocked by the question.

"Chloé, there's nothing wrong with you laughing," Vicki reassured me. "We want you to laugh. That's why we brought you here."

"If anybody is against you laughing, Chloé, they've got problems," Collette said firmly with her convincing New Jersey accent.

"You deserve to laugh again, Chloé," Angela encouraged me. "That's one of the things that I've always loved about you. You really know how to laugh. Please don't stop," she begged.

CHAPTER 12

Love on Reserve

Grief counseling was set up for our family right away. Jade and Taylor went to a counselor who specialized in children's grief while Rick and I had our own sessions with a different doctor. After three visits with the child psychologist, our precious children had been discussing among themselves what they believed was best for them and what they wanted. As Rick and I sat in the family room they came to us, holding hands. "We want to talk about Justin," they said sadly. "But not with that doctor."

At that moment and for the next several minutes my heart seemed to weigh a hundred pounds. I realized my babies were grieving in pain just like Rick and I were. I had not been there for them. I had been so engrossed in my own grief and pain over Justin that I had neglected my other children.

With a very mature attitude, they knew what they needed. "I just want to talk to my family about him," Taylor insisted. "Not to the doctor."

"Me too," Jade agreed.

It seemed a little odd, with Taylor being three years younger than Jade, that he would be the one to take the lead.

Even though Rick and I both agreed that our children needed grief counseling, we told them we understood how they felt. "How about we wait a week or two before going back? Then we can talk about it again. Okay?"

The pastoral care counselor Rick and I shared turned out to be helpful in a few areas of our lives. Yet I found that no one could really help me with getting over the loss of Justin. How could they? Sadly, my husband and I came to the conclusion that our grief was something we would have to work through on our own. We stopped going.

Several weeks after Justin's death my pain and grief turned into an unknown mixture of bereavement, anxiety, depression, and situational-induced mental illness. *How can I possibly continue to be the person I was and the person other people expect me to be? What can I do to make things better? Can things ever be better again? What about Jade and Taylor—and Rick? How can I help them? And what about* me? *Justin was* my *baby.*

The pain I felt was an oppressive weight so heavy, each night I wasn't sure I'd make it until morning. I couldn't shift it, shake it, or make it lighter. It was real. At times I literally couldn't breathe from the physical aching deep within me. It was ripping me apart. Strangely and sadly, when I visited Dr. Frank—who'd been my internist since I was twenty-five—I couldn't put my finger on the center of the pain or where it originated. I really wanted to know so I could tell him. Perhaps he'd be able to give me something to ease my suffering. Was it my heart, soul, or spirit? Or was it my mind? Many other parts of my body ached as well.

For hours on end, I would weep bitterly, only stopping when I thought about work and reminded myself that no one wanted to hire a model with swollen, red, puffy eyes—no matter how much they respected and liked her. At the end of the day, fashion was "business, Darling," as Tiziana Casoli would say. And I knew this better than most of the younger models.

I desperately needed to model. I certainly didn't need the money but what I desperately needed was the outlet. I believed this was my only passageway, my only saving grace out of my situation. I forced myself to function by working every day I could and as often as they called me with bookings.

After I had said goodnight and the children had gone to bed, the torture of my nights began. My grief was more than mental anguish. The color of my pain was maroon, red at best. It scared me. I was out of control and helpless. No one could help me.

As intelligent, savvy, and strong as I am, I couldn't help myself. I cried out loudly, "I want my baby! I just want Justin back!" I really believed if I said it long, hard, and sincerely enough, maybe God would have mercy on me and turn everything into one long nightmare. I knew God could make it so I could go to sleep and I would wake up the following morning and everything would be back to normal again.

***

Naturally, my husband was experiencing a tremendous amount of pain and grief as well. He no longer had his *baby boy*. Like any father would be, Rick was also in a very dark place. He blamed himself for what happened to Justin. Even though I tried desperately to reassure him that it was nobody's fault, he didn't buy it. He grew quiet and withdrawn.

Over the years I had become good at recognizing some of my husband's insecurities, and usually knew what to say to encourage him to move beyond them. Now he was on his own. I couldn't be there for him like I had been in the past. He would have to learn how to figure things out for himself. I cared, but I didn't have the energy to focus on anyone else.

Rick was petrified. He had been experiencing too many negative emotions, and for the first time in our marriage he couldn't lean on me. To simultaneously lose your beloved *baby boy* and the only career you've ever known was a double dose of misfortune. My husband was battling a major defeat. He was a man who to this point had believed himself to be in control and in charge of his life. Now, however, his identity as a man, a husband, a daddy, and a retired basketball player was in question. Even though he had played professionally for fifteen years, which was longer than most, his retirement had happened suddenly. At least that's how he saw it. He was not prepared and had no vision for his future. He too began to lose control. I talked about my feelings with friends. Rick, on the other hand, did not. He could not. He would not.

I held my composure for as long as I could. Long enough to accomplish my goals for Sisters Taking Action, a local group of women who desperately needed help from the community. Rick and I had promised to help them by chairing a celebrity auction event. Even though we were delayed in delivering what we promised, we were still able to keep our word and see the fundraiser through to the end.

The event was held on Justin's actual birthday, October seventeenth.

After the auction, I stayed in bed for a week. I had no bookings, nothing to make me get up out of bed. Rick did everything for the kids. All of us were in serious pain, but I didn't care about anyone else anymore. I had become completely selfish. All I cared about was my own suffering. *He was my baby. I gave birth to him. How can anyone know what I'm feeling?* It was me, me, me.

My body ached constantly. There was nothing the doctor could do for me to make me feel better. We tried several different medications and sleeping pills, and nothing worked. All I did was cry for Justin. For all I had lost. My bones hurt all the time. Rick tried to get me to eat. I couldn't. I continued to lose weight.

As the weeks passed I watched everyone around me going on with their normal lives. I was resentful and couldn't understand how they could continue as if everything was okay. Justin was gone. I began to feel numbness on one side of my body and even in my face. I was still having difficulty sleeping. I was losing my mind. Rick was tired. Jade and Taylor didn't feel stable any longer.

Rick tried to talk to me. He told me I couldn't go on like this much longer.

"I know," I cried. "But what can I do? I'm trying."

Very compassionately and with tears welling up, Rick told me in a soft, sweet voice—the voice he reserved just for me: "Chloé, please. You need to talk to the priest."

"The priest?" I screamed. "*Fuck the priest*! What the fuck does the priest know about me and what I'm feeling right now? Does he have children? Did his baby die?" I was trembling like a leaf on a tree in a storm: I saw myself about to be blown away in the wind. I was scared for my sanity, because in that moment I sincerely wanted to hurt someone else as much as I was hurting. "What can the priest do for me? *Tell me!*" I hollered out to Rick. "Tell me to go off to some fucking quiet place and read from the Psalms?"

My words were left hanging in the air while Rick's bloodshot eyes gazed back at me for at least a minute without saying a word. I could see fear and uncertainty in his face. He had no response. He began backing out of the room, walking very slowly, as though he had been dealing with a possessed woman. One he couldn't turn his back on. He returned to the kids.

Like Naomi in the Book of Ruth in the Old Testament, who had lost her husband and her sons, I had become despondent. Because I was trying to live up to what I believe others expected of me, I had been faking it so well I hadn't realized how bitter and angry I was until that moment with Rick. No one could say anything to me, or to God on my behalf, to change what had happened to Justin and my family. No one could bring my baby back.

I didn't curse God, but I guess what I'd said about the priest came pretty close. *The problem was, I didn't have anything to say to God anymore.* I had tried to read the Bible and pray but I couldn't concentrate. I felt betrayed. I believed God could have saved Justin if He had wanted to. At least He could have given me some kind of a sign he was in trouble, so I could have run to his rescue and saved him like any good and decent mother would have done. All the praying my family, friends, strangers, and I had done while Justin was in ICU was a sham. God wasn't speaking to me either. If He was talking to me, I sure couldn't hear Him. My pain became unbearable. All of my spiritual and Christian beliefs as a Roman Catholic were put through rigorous testing. Everything I had believed in to this point had to be reevaluated.

I was so afraid Rick was going to get tired of me being in such a dysfunctional state of mind, but I just couldn't help myself. I was doing the best I could. People started telling me, "Most marriages don't survive things like this, Chloé, so be careful."

The holidays rolled around. I didn't want to stay home, so we packed up and went to Aunt Anita and Uncle Arvern's for Thanksgiving. Once we were there, I became even more upset because nobody talked about Justin. I felt like they were pretending he never existed, although photographs of him were everywhere.

For Christmas we tried to make things as festive as possible for Jade and Taylor, but it was so obvious that we all missed Justin. He wasn't there to open his presents with amazement the way he had last year. I told them that it was normal for all of us to long for Justin, and that we shouldn't feel bad about missing him. Taylor and I were more open and talked about Justin often, while Rick and Jade did not. In fact, even though I had my own problems, I started to worry about Rick and Jade. They stuffed their feelings and buried everything. We managed to make it through the holidays. I'm sure it was love on reserve that got us through.

CHAPTER 13

Visitation

It was cold and unusually sunny on this particular Sunday in January. The house seemed extremely quiet even though Rick and the children were busy in the kitchen playing one of the board games they had received as a Christmas gift. I didn't want to play. I really hadn't been that much fun lately. I told them I was going to my bedroom to read. It had been four months since Justin's untimely death and I was still depressed. Lying on my bed or getting into bed alone with the covers pulled up had become typical behavior for me. On the walk through the house to my bedroom from where Rick and the kids were, I must have stopped to look at every picture of Justin I passed.

I remember those first few weeks after Justin died. Every time Rick walked past a photograph of Justin, his reaction was to turn it down so he would not have to look at his baby boy. I was just the opposite. When I walked past any of Justin's photographs I would turn them up again. Now, Rick was leaving them up as well, which made me smile. I still missed my son desperately.

I plopped down onto my bed and sighed heavily. Sitting there looking out into thin air I noticed the new books I had purchased the day before. They were stacked neatly on the sofa on the other side of the bedroom. I had been reading a lot lately and wondered which book I wanted to start now. I read the titles out loud: *"Angela's Ashes* by Frank McCourt, *It Takes a Village* by Hillary Clinton, *How Stella Got Her Groove Back* by Terry McMillan, *Her Own Rules* by Barbara Taylor Bradford,"* and a few others. It really didn't matter which one. I grabbed *Angela's Ashes* and tried to read. Everyone had been talking about this book. The reading was going well for a while and I was actually enjoying the story when I felt very sleepy. I still hadn't been sleeping well at all so I decided to let the book rest on my chest as I tried to give in to a much-needed nap.

Slowly, I was drifting off to sleep. Just as I found myself enjoying sleep, I was awakened by what felt like someone jumping up and down on the bed. Jade had never jumped on the bed before, so immediately I thought it was Taylor. I rolled over to tell him to stop. But Taylor wasn't there. No one was there. *That's strange*, I thought. I drifted right back off to sleep. Seconds later, the jumping began again. This time my heart told me, *"It's Justin's spirit."*

I opened my eyes to get a look at him but he wasn't there—just the jumping. Justin loved our bed; in fact, he could jump up and down on it for hours. He knew this aggravated me enormously but he was willing to take his chances. Sometimes Justin would sneak into our room and pull himself up on our bed and jump, jump, jump away, until his little heart was content. Then he would call his daddy with a mischievous smile on his cute little angel face.

When Rick got there and saw the disheveled bed Justin would point to the bed and laugh hysterically, running right into Rick's arms. "Mommy's bed," he would say. Knowing good and well he should not have done what he did.

I'd hear Rick tell him, "Mommy's gon' spank your butt about jumping on her bed." Justin just laughed, not believing a word his daddy said.

Realizing what was happening I instinctively closed my eyes again and relaxed for the first time in months, enjoying Justin's presence. He continued to jump. I knew he was smiling and laughing. Although he didn't make a sound, my spirit knew. We were connected—spirit to spirit. I perceived Justin moving from the bed to the floor right by the foot of my side of the bed. There was a metal emblem bedpost, which began to spin around. Justin always did that. It seemed as though he put his foot on the rail, then pulled himself up as he had done so many times before. Now, he was back on the bed. I could feel the wind from his spirit all around me. It was bold yet mild and sweet. I felt a gentle breeze around my face and at one point Justin was kissing me on both cheeks the way he had kissed me thousands of times before. He jumped up and down on the bed two or three times more, and was gone. I waited a little while to see if he might come back. He did not.

With incredible ease and with an enormous sense of peace I felt a genuine smile break free. I felt lighter than I ever had since the day Justin fell in the pool. What I experienced was ethereal yet positively real and powerful. I knew I would never be able to fully explain this encounter in words, but I sure wanted to try.

I got up from my slumber and nearly floated down the hall into the kitchen. I needed to share this wonderful and absolutely amazing experience with Rick and the children. They all noticed my smile. It was indeed something to notice. Justin's visitation must have left a glimpse of heaven on my face when he kissed me on my cheeks.

"What are you smiling for, Mommy?" Jade wanted to know right away. It had been a while since they had seen me smile genuinely. I told them what had happened. I tried explaining it—that my spirit had been with Justin's spirit, and that even though I did not see him, I had a whole-body perception. I didn't have to convince them. They believed me right away and gathered around me with sweetness and love. At that very moment it was all about *love*.

Rick, Jade, and Taylor had many questions for me. I tried to answer all of them as best I could but I just didn't have the language to fully explain. I finally said, "There is no way I can even begin to answer all of your questions because I really don't understand it myself. I've heard about similar experiences, but this is out of this world." I told them I needed to talk to the people at church about it before I would fully understand. "But this is what I feel in my spirit: Justin is wonderful. His spirit is with God. He wanted me to know he is happy and well, and that he will always be our angel in heaven."

With that said, we all stood in the kitchen hugging, holding each other and doing our happy dance, praising God for such a wonderful gift.

After we settled down, Rick confessed, smiling warmly at me, "I wish something like that would happen to me."

For the next several days all I could think about was my spiritual experience with Justin. It was undeniable. This had not been the only spiritual adventure I had ever been on personally, but it certainly was the most powerful.

***

About a year before Justin died, I heard angelic music, which I believe came from heaven. It sounded like thousands of voices harmonizing. It was on a beautiful sunny afternoon and I had fallen asleep reading, just as it had happened that day in January after his death. While sleeping, I heard bold, beautiful, unfamiliar music. My radio wasn't set for a station that would play music like that, nor did I have any tapes or CDs with that type of music. Naturally, with two rambunctious boys in the house I thought one of them had come into my bedroom and turned on the radio. I reached over with my eyes still closed to turn it off. While fumbling with it I was surprised because I couldn't find the switch to turn it off. At that moment I heard: *Music like this does not come from the radio.*

This soothing voice resonated within me and right away I believed it. I had such a wonderful feeling. I was caught up in a situation over which I had no control. Everything around me was golden. But the light was *inside* of me—not from the sun outside. I felt as though I levitated from my bed. I was aware that I was in my bedroom but at the same time I was also someplace else. The feeling was awesome. It was effervescent, light, and loving. When the experience was over I wanted desperately to know how long this had lasted. Was it for a minute? Five minutes? Or thirty minutes? Time seemed to have stopped.

This experience took a lot out of me but at the same time I had been filled up with something good. It was LOVE. *What had happened to me?* I wanted to figure this out, but *how?* I asked myself. *How can I share this with anyone if I can't fully explain it myself?* It had definitely been celestial.

One day I found the courage to share my experience with a friend. Her reaction was to explain it away chemically, telling me that my brain had done it by firing off neurons and chemicals I could not grasp. Another friend laughed and dismissed it with a wave of her hand. Others were intrigued and wanted to know more. Nevertheless, they still looked at me side-eyed. But Aunt Shirley was different. The day I spoke with her I had no intention of talking about my experience. However, when it came up, she didn't hesitate in her thoughts. She said, "Oh! You were with Jesus."

"What?" I laughed. Now I was the one who thought *she* was strange.

"Why is this so hard for you to believe?" she asked.

I couldn't answer her. When our conversation ended and I hung up the phone, I wasn't laughing anymore. *Could this be possible? Could I have been with Jesus?*

Several months passed. One day while reading Scripture I came across something quite profound—something that made me reflect on what Aunt Shirley had said about me being with Jesus. It was in Second Corinthians, Chapter 12. I read about an experience the Apostle Paul had. He said he had been "caught up to the third heaven." He said, "Whether it was in the body or out of the body I do not know—God knows." Paul also said he "was caught up to paradise." And he "heard inexpressible things."

"If this could happen to Saint Paul, to another human being, why not to me?" I asked Rick.

He wasn't sure. "Did God lift me up to share a glimpse of heaven with me?" I asked.

The music and everything else that happened to me on that particular day was literally indescribable. I believe that because of this earlier experience, it was instinctive for me to welcome Justin's spirit when it arrived. I was so grateful. It opened the door for our family to start healing. Justin wanted me to know that he was better than good; that his spirit was the same as it had always been; and that he was continuing right on with his purpose.

This was indeed a gift that had come from the Spirit of God. God had given it to me and *I accepted it*. I understood it and knew it was not foolishness. I finally had something to go on, and I knew God was real. Even though I had been extremely angry with God and couldn't possibly understand why Justin had to die, on the other hand I still couldn't deny all the things God had done for me in the past. All the things He had done to help me survive and grow. All the things He had brought me through.

After several days of reflecting on my past and realizing all the good God had done for me, I came to the conclusion that Justin was safe. He was happy and in God's hands. I believe that Justin wanted me to know he was in heaven and would always be our angel. I believe his spirit returned to me and jumped on the bed, as only he could, to personally let his mommy know. At this moment it seemed right that I would declare to myself and to God that I wanted to be whole again. I made the decision to be happy. To live, to love, and to laugh. "Please God," I prayed earnestly. "Just let me laugh again." I wanted my deep hearty laugh back, the laugh that could move others, the laugh that encouraged me and comforted so many, the laugh that filled me up and healed me. I finally realized: *Living a life without laughter is no life at all*.

By sending Justin's spirit to me, God had given me the green light to go ahead and live my life full out again. It was up to me now to be happy. No one else could do this for me. I decided I needed to do something different, to change some things in my life.

I made a decision that day to change my inner world: I wanted to change my thinking, and the way I had been looking at my life. I decided to change a few things about my *outer* world, too. I switched from L'Agence Models to Click Models. I loved my friends at L'Agence, especially Mark and Madeleine, but it was time to move forward. I called Chicago to tell my agency there that I was available for direct bookings. I decided I needed to get out of Atlanta as often as possible.

Paolo and Manu, our friends from Milan, called from Italy to ask us to meet them in Miami for a week. Rick and I were very excited. We hadn't seen our friends for nearly two years, and we were absolutely ready for a vacation.

Rick and I had met Paolo our first month living in Italy. At the time none of us had children yet, so we all enjoyed our fast-paced, jet-set lifestyle. Just the thought of hanging out with these guys again exhilarated us. We could hardly wait.

The Florida sun was awesome. It made a world of difference. The first night, we dined at an Italian restaurant in South Beach that reminded us of Milan. Not because of the food or the ambience, but because of all the Italians we ran into, who were acquaintances of Paolo and Manu. Paolo joked that just being with us again made him want to drink several bottles of champagne, as we'd done in our younger days. Of course, each of us had grown older and wiser and knew one bottle was plenty.

The trip to Miami was just what Rick and I needed. We'd fallen in love all over again and started getting our groove back. After we returned to Atlanta we saw things differently. We wanted so much for our family; but we also realized we still had to take it one day at a time. After coming home from Florida, we had lots of energy and truly wanted to be happy again—really happy, not just going through the motions and faking it. We knew both sides and we wanted happy-happy!

We didn't try to fool ourselves, however. We knew we would always long for Justin, and that sad feelings about his accident and untimely death could still arise without warning. But nevertheless we were very hopeful things could *and would* get better.

We decided together that we had to do the best we could. I tried to think of anything to get out of the house when I wasn't working and the children were in school. I still didn't want to be there alone for extended periods of time. I created different projects for myself to stay busy, and I started writing.

Sometimes it was difficult to be happy. Nevertheless, I knew that *my decision to be happy* kept me going. It was daily practice, and I had to remind myself each day—and sometimes each hour   of my decision to laugh again. We started watching comedies on television and going to fun movies.

***

In April, a friend tricked me into going on a weekend spiritual retreat. After I completed the full experience, I was so glad she did. The solitude was incredibly rejuvenating. We celebrated morning and evening mass. We were allowed to speak only during confessions and Spiritual Direction. When I went in to make my confession I had no idea I was going to bring up so many issues from my past. It was gut wrenching—so much so that Father Larry, the priest who heard my confession, cried almost as much as I did.

"Chloé, you *must* forgive them," he urged me through his tears. Father Larry as well as Father John, a priest who was also there and had been a big part of my life previously, helped me to refocus and set spiritual goals. As a result of their help and support, I realized God was perfecting me and getting me ready for something I didn't understand right away. They assured me it would be revealed to me. All I needed to do, they said, was *Keep your eyes on The Lord*.

A week after I returned from my retreat, Taylor received his first Holy Communion. It was a big deal for our entire family. All of his aunts and uncles came to see him. Monsignor O'Conner, our pastor who had been a part of lives from the beginning of our marriage, wanted to take pictures with Taylor and our family. He told us how well we were doing, adding in his melodic voice, "Remember, you're blessed." I knew we were. Even though the pain of losing Justin was still there, the blessings were obvious everywhere we looked.

The following week, Jade and Taylor both received awards for having perfect attendance at religious education classes. Everyone seemed impressed that they hadn't missed one single night, considering what had happened in our family.

By May, I was feeling triumphant. I knew I was going to make it. I set out to create my life based on what God had given me. I knew God still wanted me to have a wonderful life. God wanted me to be happy. He wanted me to laugh again.

CHAPTER 14

Restoration

It had almost been a year since my spiritual retreat. What I had learned since then was immeasurable. The decision Rick and I had made to go on with our lives and be happy was the first step. But it certainly wasn't the last. It didn't take the pain away, but it did give us a new focus. Some days were really wonderful; others were good; some turned out to be as difficult as the first days had been. The realization that God was getting me ready for something gave me hope and strength. I grew impatient. I desperately wanted to know my purpose.

Over the last year I had made the greatest spiritual leap of my entire life. I discovered I had a yearning—a deep unquenchable thirst for The Father, The Son, and The Holy Spirit. I went to mass several times a week, read the Bible, read spiritual books, and listened to messages on tapes and Christian radio stations. I couldn't get enough. I shared everything with Rick and he absorbed as much as he could. He had reverence for what God was teaching me.

On Memorial Day weekend, when Rick and the kids were visiting his father in Mississippi, my friend Bobby Jo and I relaxed on my deck. She had made it her mission to stick by me. "I watched a wonderful Easter program on TV last month from Mount Paran Church," she told me. "We should go tomorrow to visit." She knew I wasn't big on visiting other folks' churches, so she watched carefully for my reaction.

"What kind of church is Mount Paran?" I inquired skeptically. I had my own church and I was good with that. *What's the point in church hopping?*

"I don't know, Chloé," she replied, slightly irritated. "Sometimes you just need to loosen up a little bit, Girl. Try different things."

She leaned in closer to me with her brows arched and a silly smirk on her face. "Remember, Chloé, you didn't want to listen to those Bishop T. D. Jakes tapes of mine either, did you? Now I can't even get them back!"

I couldn't say a word. She was right. I agreed to go. I had indeed been enjoying her Bishop Jakes tapes.

Mount Paran Church of God in Atlanta was like no other church I had ever attended anywhere. Dr. David Cooper, the animated senior pastor, was truly a teacher kind of preacher. Eloquent, knowledgeable, and lively, he seemed anointed to inspire, teach, and share God's Word. He made me laugh and cry as I learned how to really *praise* and *worship* The Lord. This has been one of the most valuable gifts I have ever received. I have to give my girlfriend and God credit for that day, the day I began the next phase of my spiritual transformation and life journey.

***

In early June, my cousin Vicki called to ask me about my plans for my fortieth birthday. "Isn't this the big one coming up?" She wanted to know. I could tell she was grinning.

"I don't want to do anything."

"Maybe that's because you're getting elderly," she said sarcastically.

If it had been anyone else, I would have been livid; but I knew she only wanted me to laugh and have some fun.

"I'll think about it," I told her. The truth was, I didn't believe I deserved a party. Not yet.

***

A few weeks later, gigantic gray clouds blew into Atlanta and our whole neighborhood lost power. Rick and I played board games with Jade and Taylor for hours. Then, out of the blue I began to grow weary. The reality of our lives had suddenly become unclear to me. *Where were we headed*? Becoming so uncertain so abruptly left me with a heavy sinking feeling. Just as the excitement of the children being cozy with Mommy and Daddy all day long playing games began to wear off, the lights began to flicker, giving us hope we would have light again soon. Finally, we had our electricity back. We'd been without power for seven hours.

The power for our home returned, but not mine. Over the last year and a half I'd learned some techniques to push away the depression I felt coming. Writing was one of them. Since I knew writing had become cathartic for me, I went to my home office to write. However, sitting at my computer trying to force myself to write made me more anxious and even more uncertain of myself. Justin's photograph sat on my desk. He looked right into my eyes with a smile that told me, "You can do it Mommy!"

I held the photograph up close to my heart, not wanting to give in to the feelings that threatened to overpower me.

Why is this happening now? No answer came, only more despair.

I kept my feelings to myself. I didn't want to bring my family down. I knew whatever mood or persona I took on would affect them as well. After thirty minutes of feeling as though I was sinking and about to drown myself, I knew the only thing that could possibly rescue me from this abyss was to get up, go into my dressing room, and *pray.*

When I entered the dressing room it was as though I'd left *myself* behind at the computer. At this moment I had no power, no wisdom of my own. I barely had strength enough to walk. I was helpless and could no longer rely on myself. I took an old, beat-up Bible into the dressing room with me. Strangely, I'd found it several years earlier lying on the side of the street in front of my house with its pages flipping and blowing in the wind. *You don't just see a Bible lying on the ground in front of your house and leave it there, Chloé.* I brought it home with me. For three years I left this Bible in the bottom drawer of the kitchen desk until I began visiting Mount Paran. Turns out, it was the *New International Version*—the version Dr. Cooper read from during his sermons.

Everyone brought their Bibles to church there, unlike at St. Jude's, my family's church. Bobby Jo, my friend who introduced me to Mount Paran, laughed when she saw me carrying this particular Bible

Chloe Taylor Brown

"Now this is the kind of Bible you can hold up and shake in people's faces, Girl," she laughed, wagging it in my face.

I knew what she meant. "With such a well-worn, dog-eared Bible," she joked, "you can carry the authority of a street preacher, Girl!"

This old Bible had become a refuge for me. When I picked it up from the street that Sunday afternoon I knew at the time there was something special about it. However, it had taken me years to figure out why: It was a study Bible, with sections that explained everything I read, indicating where to find background information. In other words, it took me on many biblical explorations. I couldn't get enough. It was giving me peace and understanding. Most importantly, I was learning how to apply the principles of Scripture to my everyday life.

Crossing the threshold into my dressing room, I forgot the proud self I had been, and entered with humility. Being humble seem to give me a little more energy and made me stronger. I threw my body down on the floor and clutched my old new-favorite Bible. I didn't know what I was going to pray about or what I was going to read or say. I began to praise and worship The Lord the way I learned at Mount Paran, thanking God for my life, my family, and all the things in my life.

"Your grace has carried me for so long. I need You now, Lord." I didn't want to return to despair. I cried out to God again, pleading with Him to help me. "Show me what *You* want for my life and for my family," I cried and begged.

During all of those hours I'd listened to Bishop T. D. Jakes on tape I recalled him saying, "The Holy Spirit pours

136

out what you have prayed *in*." He also had said, "You have to get the Word of God down inside you, so The Holy Spirit can bring it to your remembrance when you need it."

As I lay there on the floor with tears streaming down my face I cried out again. "God, please forgive me! Help me!" Just as Bishop Jakes said, The Holy Spirit immediately brought to my remembrance a Bible verse I knew: *If My people, who are called by My Name, will humble themselves and pray, and seek My face, and turn from their wicked ways, then will I hear from heaven, and I will heal their land.* I did not have to strain my ear to catch the wondrous words that were spoken to me this late summer afternoon. They seemed not to come to me through my ears, but directly into my soul and spirit. Ferociously I turned the leaves of my worn Bible. I searched to find these words in The Old Testament. I found them already highlighted in orange. I had read it several times before, and it seemed to be waiting for me in Second Chronicles, Chapter 7, verse 14. I read God's words again. I prayed and humbled myself.

I asked God in the name of Jesus to direct us. "What should we do about our house?" Our living expenses were enormous and we had very little money coming in. We needed to make some serious decisions. "But this is—was—Justin's home" I protested. "This is where he was born, lived, and died," I reasoned. "Why do I really want to continue staying here, Lord?" I pleaded for an answer. "What's the best thing for my family? What's the best thing for me?"

I finally told God, "I'm offering everything up to You, so You have to take over."

At this moment I had peace. I began to feel the tension drain from my shoulders as I instinctively inhaled deeply and exhaled slowly several times. As I was stretched out on the floor I placed my face into the thin strong pages of my Bible and let them absorb my tears until they stopped and dried up.

Relieved and feeling refreshed, I got up slowly to gather myself. I walked back into my office and returned to my computer as though nothing had happened. I don't know if Rick or the children ever noticed I had left my desk. No one came looking for me for nearly an hour, which was unusual. They always needed me for one reason or another.

As I sat at my computer trying to position myself again to write, Rick saw me and came in. "Hey, what's up?" he asked, not waiting for an answer. "I'm getting ready to leave. I need to check on a couple of my accounts." He had recently purchased a new business that I knew very little about. The look in his eye and the feelings I sensed from him told me he was worried about our finances.

I asked him what was wrong, but he didn't answer.

"Baby, maybe you should go pray," I suggested. He said he would.

Rick and I didn't share prayer space. He went upstairs to pray. After about fifteen minutes, he came downstairs to tell me, "I'll see you in a few hours, Baby."

"Do you feel better?" I asked him.

He said yes, but I was not convinced. He leaned over my desk and gave me a half-hearted peck on the cheek and left the house.

Even though I was now concerned about Rick, I did feel more at ease myself. I didn't feel as heavy and blue as I had felt before going into my prayer closet. I was now able to write, and believed Rick would feel better when he got back later in the evening. As I sat there immersed in my own words on my computer screen, the phone rang. It startled and annoyed me a bit. I had just begun to flow again.

"Hello," I said quickly wanting to get rid of the person on the other end of the phone.

"Hello," a hesitant voice responded.

"My name is David." The caller told me his brother had just built a new house. His brother's new next-door neighbors had been our old neighbors and our children's swimming friends. They had just moved there from our neighborhood a few weeks earlier and they'd told him we might want to sell our house.

"Our house is not on the market to be sold." I told him, truly bothered by his interruption. However, as soon as the word *sold* left my lips, I remembered my prayers. I had just asked God to make it plain and clear to me about what we should do about the house!

Maybe this *is the answer*! I thought. While all of this was going on in my head, the man never stopped talking. He finally got around to asking, "May I see your home?"

"Yes." I said, thinking it might be a good opportunity, and I could make arrangements for them to come over later during the week. However, the man and his wife were calling from our gate phone. They were sitting right in front of our home, looking at the house from the top of the driveway. Rick had just left but at this point there was no hesitation or fear. I buzzed them in!

***

David and Belinda were indeed an answer to my prayer. Rick and I prepared ourselves to sell our dream home. I truly adored it. We all did; but it was time to go. We knew all the memories of Justin would live forever in our hearts but it was time to move forward according to God's plan.

Feeling at peace with my path I was ready to celebrate my birthday and my journey through life. Vicki and her new husband, John, took us to Chastain Park, a wonderful outdoor amphitheater in Atlanta, to see Al Jarreau in concert. Of course it was a fabulous evening. We enjoyed a five-star meal by candlelight as we sipped fine champagne.

Only four weeks after we'd met David and his wife Belinda, we had the check in our hands. They had previously sold their house before moving to Atlanta, and they paid us in cash. "We have the money just sitting there in our bank, so we may as well go ahead and let it sit in your bank while you guys look for a new house," David reasoned.

We told them, "You have a deal!" The house was sold. We were free to move anywhere we wanted. The thing that is so amazing to me about selling our house is that it happened without much effort. God aligned it up perfectly, right after Rick and I both prayed that day.

We sold the house and had nowhere to move to because everything happened so very quickly. "Don't worry about that," David assured us. You guys weren't expecting to sell your house, so take your time. We're very comfortable at my brother's house for right now."

Rick and I soon found a beautiful new house that would become our home. It was a little further out of Atlanta than we were accustomed to, but we already knew we would adjust nicely. The house was being built and in its last stages of completion. The builder assured us they would soon be finished with everything and we could be in within five weeks from the day we signed the contract.

***

It was the beginning of our new life adventure. While Jade and Taylor were in summer camp again, Rick and I took the opportunity to visit Collette in New York. I had not seen my friend in months and genuinely missed her. On this visit to New York City we remembered how to relax, and we also remembered how to party. The three of us had been friends since 1982 after meeting during Rick's Golden State Warrior basketball days. Collette's former husband had been Rick's teammate.

Upon returning to Atlanta we learned that our new house would be delayed for another two weeks before it was finished. We believed David and Belinda would understand and allow us to stay for an additional two weeks but we had given them our word and needed to pack up and move. I thought of my girlfriend Bobby Jo, who lived in a mansion near the neighborhood where we were going to be moving. I told her our situation and about the new closing date.

"Y'all come on!" she said without hesitation. We packed up our beloved home, sent most of our furniture and personal belongings to storage, and packed up the car and the van with the children and the dog. Unfortunately, we soon found out about unexpected delays—things that could go wrong with even the best builders. I was livid when I got the news from the realtor.

"Don't worry about it, Chloé," Bobby Jo told me, "because when y'all leave that will be it. We're gonna put all of this behind us and still be friends." She giggled and looked at me sideways.

I decided to let it go, and quietly opened the back door to step outside and sit on her patio. Even though it was the end of August, there was a cool tropical breeze blowing. As I relaxed my head on the back of the overstuffed lawn chair, I inhaled deeply to fill my lungs with the fragrant summer air, and exhaled slowly. There was just enough golden sunlight left to smile down on me through the lush green trees in her backyard. As I tilted my face toward the sun to absorb the rays I instinctively brought my hand up to adjust my sunglasses—sunglasses Giorgio Armani had personally given to me after his 1988 Fall Prêt-à-Porter Spring Collection in Milan, Italy. Ironically, I believed it was the last fashion show I would ever do in Milan.

Memories from that era of my life started to flash before me again in living color and with all the original voices and sound bites. My feelings were mixed. I couldn't tell if I felt happy or sad about it, and decided to be merely a keen observer. I watched it all like a movie in my mind. A tear fell to my cheek as I remembered the highs and lows of my life.

Of all the hurdles I have jumped in my life, the death of my son certainly has been the highest—the most difficult challenge by far. The path on such rocky terrain has led me through deep valleys of grief and suffering. On the other hand, I have also reached pinnacles on several occasions, where I have had great moments of self-actualization. I have worked and traveled, and seen and done things most people only dream about. I am fortunate and blessed to have experienced and enjoyed immense love and affection from my husband.

"Girl, you sho' look relaxed," Bobby Jo drawled as she pulled up a chair to join me on the patio.

"Where're the kids?" Restless, she answered her own question with a question. "They must be with Rick, huh?"

Not wanting to have my moment of solitude interrupted, I reluctantly nodded, hoping she'd get the message and leave me to my reverie. She didn't. She wanted to talk. I felt indebted to my hostess, so I indulged her.

Bobby Jo and I had been friends since college. We met at Mississippi State University just weeks after our first semester began. She and my husband were from the same town, and it was she who had introduced me to Rick a few months after we had become friends that first year of college. Bobby Jo and I have similar values, but we're as different as night and day. Intelligent, gregarious, competitive, eccentric, and generous, she was now divorced with one son who was two months younger than my son Taylor.

She shifted her weight in the lawn chair, and adjusted her sunglasses. "Chloé!" She called my name, even though I was less than a foot away. "We should all go out more and have a little more *fun*, Girl."

She waited for me to respond but I didn't. "Especially you and Rick," she added. "Y'all startin' to act kinda *old*, child."

We both burst out into a hearty laugh that got bigger and bigger. We laughed so hard and long, we couldn't seem to stop. Bobby Jo started crying from the sheer pleasure of our laughter. Her tears were ruining her make-up.

When we finally caught our breath, she said, "Chloé, it sho' feels good to laugh, don't it, Girl?

CHAPTER 15
I Know Something

I had given up fashion shows a year or so earlier, but when the fashion booker from Click Models phoned me, she caught me off-guard. "Chloé, Jeffrey wants to book you for his show." Jeffrey really knew how to make a fashion show an Event with a capital E. His show, Jeffrey Fashion Cares, is Atlanta's premier fashion show of the year, which always kicks off the fall fashion season. As in previous years, the proceeds would benefit Jeffrey's favorite charities. Because he insisted on hiring the city's top fashion models, everyone in the fashion business and the local press would attend to contribute to the cause, as well as to see what Jeffery would do this year. I was happy to take the job.

It was five o'clock on the day of the show. I had one hour to get my model's bag together and get to the Theatre in Buckhead where the show was being held this year. I was excited about seeing all my model girlfriends and other friends in the local industry. Several of them had called to tell me they had seen my name and photograph on the storyboard lineup. They said they couldn't wait to see me. I was the first model to arrive at the theater, which was so unlike me. I decided to relax and wait. As the first few young girls arrived, some of whom I had trained, they came up to me to say hello and give me a hug.

Jeffrey finally made his entrance. Spotting me immediately he came right over and kissed me on both cheeks. "Chloé, I'm putting you in the long, slinky, animal-print dress," he sang in a slow, slightly Southern tone.

"You and Tami are the only girls who know how to walk like a real woman in that dress, Girl." He went on to say, "I gave it to *you*, though, because your shoulders are to die for." I laughed happily at Jeffrey as he walked away with exaggerated steps.

I spotted a few of my friends and rushed over. We reconnected instantly by picking up right where we left off last time, and other girls filled me in. We caught up on all the gossip in town and told each other how fabulous we all looked. We talked about make-up and hairstyles, boyfriends, husbands, and children. It was wonderful catching up and giggling like schoolgirls.

"Girls, it's time for rehearsal!"

We instantly became seasoned divas. *Show time, Darling!*

***

We finally closed the deal on our new home in October. *Nine weeks* past our original closing date. Just a few days before we moved in, we strolled together through the new neighborhood. Since we had been there in the area almost every day for the last two months, it already felt like home. This transition had not been ideal, but the four of us were moving on as a family. As a team.

Walking a few feet ahead, Taylor stopped suddenly and turned to face us. With the purity of a child's wisdom he summed up our gratitude for our good fortune.

"God sure hooked us up, didn't He, Daddy?"

***

We adored our new home. For the first time we felt great about living in a subdivision in the suburbs. I was finally settled. The house was beautiful, and everything was flowing well as we started to get excited about the holidays.

On the afternoon of December fifteenth, while taking a long, hot, relaxing shower, I received a spiritual message that further confirmed I was on the right path. I had been in a light and jovial mood all day long. The kids had three more days before their Christmas break. I was trying to unwind as much as possible to get ready for the Christmas rush. The hot water was relaxing. My mind was peaceful and clear. As the soothing water ran down my shoulders I received a message from The Holy Spirit: *Everything will be restored unto you.*

I didn't question the message. I believed and accepted it. Standing still in the shower, I could perceive the experience in every inch of my body. It was another whole body felt perception. I had no idea what God had in store for me, but I knew it was going to be good.

The Christmas holiday season began beautifully. I had a feeling of euphoria as I was surrounded by love. Even though I was not able to articulate what "*Everything will be restored unto you*" meant, the message brought me peace.

I shared it only with Rick the next day, and then also with Collette, who had come for a visit toward the end of the holidays.

***

We brought the New Year in with a glorious bang—and champagne! It was January first, 1999, and all I could do was praise God and play the song *1999* by Prince, and dance! On January tenth, Rick and I awoke with a strong feeling that it was time to visit Mount Paran Church. We still enjoyed visiting this church particularly because of Dr. Cooper's teaching. And it was a really cool church to praise and worship. It was surely *spirit-filled*, as we had learned.

That Sunday, after all of the great singing ended, the praise and worship continued. The choir director headed to his seat, and Dr. Cooper walked over and stood at the podium, with his hands still up, praising God. He was about to preach the sermon. Suddenly, a man way up in the second-floor balcony of the congregation started speaking boldly and loudly in a different language. They called it *speaking in tongues*. The church fell silent immediately. You could hear a pin drop. Everyone who heard the man listened intently. I know I did. Dr. Cooper bowed his head as he listened further to what the man had to share.

When Dr. Cooper finally lifted his head, he told the congregation, "I have a message for everyone here today from The Holy Spirit."

"Each one of you will think this message is particularly for you, but in fact, it is for the whole church."

He said, "The Holy Spirit wants me to tell you that everything you have lost will be restored unto you in 1999."

Before Dr. Cooper even finished, I felt chills. A phenomenal tingling sensation filled me from my head to my toes. Instantly I felt and *knew* I was pregnant. It was an *absolute* knowing. Sitting there Rick and I reached for each other's hands. We were present as one and looked deep into each other's eyes. He nodded *yes* to me as the service continued. We could not speak but both of us had a flood of emotions.

Dr. Cooper told us this had never happened before, and that there was no need for him to preach the message he'd prepared. The message came through the man in the balcony in a different language from the Holy Spirit, and it was translated by Dr. Cooper. According to him, *that* was the sermon and the message for the whole church for that day. The service was dismissed.

We finally got back to our car after the service. I could hardly wait, so I hurriedly asked Rick, "Baby, what did you mean when you nodded to me in church?"

Rick was as wound up as I was. "When Dr. Cooper translated the message from the man speaking in tongues, I thought about Justin, and believed God was telling us we were going to have another baby!"

"Baby! *Really*? Me too!" I told Rick what I'd felt earlier.

We shared our feelings with Jade and Taylor. We were very excited.

Coincidentally the next day was my yearly physical, which had been scheduled three months earlier.

"Hello Mrs. Brown," my doctor greeted me. How have you been?"

"Hi there! I'm doing very well. Thanks."

As we carried on with the usual routine OB/GYN talk, I asked for a pregnancy test.

She looked up from her clipboard and asked, "A pregnancy test? Do you feel pregnant?"

"No, I don't. I just want a test."

The technician drew my blood and told me, "You'll receive a phone call with the results tomorrow."

The next day I waited at home for that phone call all day long. Eventually I had to leave for an errand. Naturally, that's when the call came. I had already given them permission to leave a message with Rick or on the answering machine if I was not there to take the call personally. When I walked in the door, Rick and Taylor were standing in the middle of the kitchen grinning from ear to ear.

Bursting with excitement, Taylor piped up, "Mommy, I know something!" He didn't wait for me to ask what. "You're pregnant!" I'll never forget how beautiful and funny it was to hear the news of my pregnancy from my almost-ten-year-old son.

Jade walked into the house five minutes later from school. Taylor couldn't wait, announcing the news even before she could put down her book bag. Jade was so elated, she let her heavy book bag fall to the floor. We immediately gathered in a circle as we always do when we hear good news. We held hands, jumping up and down with joy, and shouting, *Praise The Lord!*

***

I've learned that God has the power to make good from any bad thing. No matter what happens in my life, I know God is in control, and I will continue to trust in Him. I know He wants me to encourage and help other people. Most importantly, *God wants me to laugh again.* God is on my side, and Justin is with Him.

Every day, I remind myself: *In the end, God always wins.*

Chloé praying and praising The Lord

EPILOGUE

Especially For Chloé and Rick

by Carl A. Lee

Sometimes our burdens are carried by
LOVE to a spiritual space
We recognize the redeeming power of unconditional GRACE
Accept sunshine as the face of GOD—
let go of your worries and fears
Stop counting the pains and gains—our troubles and tears
Suddenly surrender simply to the flow
Allow the water—by faith—to cleanse our hearts as we go
Use our wings fitted by MERCY without measure
Realize through it all our journey is the treasure
In GRATITUDE to everything big and small or in between
Finally, know the understanding we've been
given was by us sought and seen

Edwards Brothers Malloy
Oxnard, CA USA
January 22, 2016